STORIES OF THOSE WHO
ENCOUNTERED JESUS

NEVER THE SAME

STEVEN JAMES

ZONDERVAN™

GRAND RAPIDS, MICHIGAN 49530 USA

invert

www.invertbooks.com

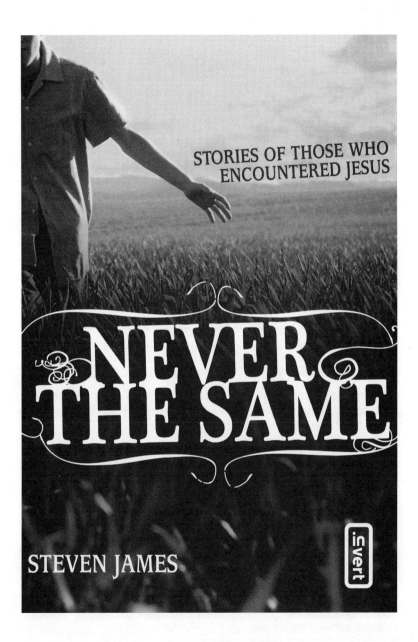

STORIES OF THOSE WHO
ENCOUNTERED JESUS

NEVER THE SAME

STEVEN JAMES

.isvert

invert

Never the Same: Stories of Those Who Encountered Jesus
Copyright © 2005 by Youth Specialties

Youth Specialties Products, 300 South Pierce Street, El Cajon, CA 92020, are published by
Zondervan, 5300 Patterson Avenue SE, Grand Rapids, MI 49530

Library of Congress Cataloging-in-Publication Data

James, Steven, 1969-
  Never the same : stories of those who encountered Jesus / by Steven James.
    p. cm.
  ISBN 0-310-25951-7 (pbk.)
  1. Jesus Christ--Person and offices--Juvenile literature. 2. Jesus
Christ--Friends and associates--Juvenile literature. I. Title.
  BT203.J36 2005
  232.9'5--dc22

2004030062

Editorial direction by Doug Davidson
Editing by Kristi Robison
Proofreading by Janie Wilkerson
Interior design by Mark Novelli - Imago Media
Cover Design by Burnkit
Printed in the United States of America

05 06 07 08 09 10 / DCI / 10 9 8 7 6 5 4 3 2 1

table of contents

Thanks to Liesl, Sonya, Pam, Jeff, Dana, Esther, and Ashley
for your thoughts and suggestions and to Pamela, Jay, and Doug
for your encouragement and guidance.

for Terry Maughon,
who has introduced so many teens to the Mystery

"In the end, however, when people ask me, 'What made you a follower of the
Master?' I can only answer: the Master."
—Sundar Singh (1889-1929),
Indian spiritual leader who converted to Christianity when he was 16 years old

introduction

"Who do you say I am?"- Jesus of Nazareth (Luke 9:20)

What would it have been like to meet Jesus face to face? To listen to him tell story after story around a glimmering campfire? To trudge with him along the dusty roads of Galilee? To feel him good-naturedly slap your shoulder after telling a joke? To see the look in his eyes when he talked about his Father? To glide your fingers across the ugly scar on his hand? To bow at his feet in a moment of stillness and worship?

Jesus was the ultimate mystery man—*Rabbi. Rebel. Teacher. Healer. Poet. Prophet. King. Questioner. Storyteller. Light of the World. Friend of Those in Darkness. Miracle Worker. Condemned Heretic. Philosopher. Carpenter. Messiah. The Guy Next Door. The God of the Universe. The Son of Man. The Son of God.*

There was nothing normal about him, and everything normal about him. He fit in effortlessly yet stood out magnificently. He was a living paradox. When Jesus was born, the eternal became temporary. The king of all became the slave of everyone. The light of life entered the valley of the shadow of death and transformed it forever.

And no one really knew what to make of him. Some thought he was a dangerous terrorist (John 11:48; Luke 23:14). Others said he was possessed by demons (Matthew 9:34). His own family thought he was certifiably crazy (Mark 3:21). A few people believed he was actually the long-awaited, one and only Savior of the human race (Matthew 16:16; Acts 4:12).

The apostle Paul called Jesus "the mystery of God . . . in whom are hidden all the treasures of wisdom and knowledge" (Colossians 2:2-3). Did you catch that? To find true wisdom you need to enter through a mystery. Meeting the Mystery is the key to finding the truth about life.

Jesus is an ocean spilling over its banks in a raging storm, a sea so calm it holds the sky in its heart, a river gaining momentum as it tumbles down the mountain. He engulfs and untangles, bewilders and clarifies, mystifies, frees, and astounds.

Lord. Parable. Riddle. Savior. Mystery.

Jesus.

And one thing is certain. When people meet him, they're never the same again. Their lives are changed forever.

In this book you'll meet some of those people. Sometimes we know their names; sometimes we don't. Sometimes we know how their stories ended; sometimes they've disappeared into the sands of time. In every case, though, the stories you're about to read are based on actual, true events. All of these storytellers met the Story himself.

As I've retold these stories, I've taken incidents or moments from the life of Jesus and tried to get into the heads of the characters involved. In some stories much of the material is drawn directly from Scripture. Other stories are more speculative. I've added details and dialogue to make it easier to see and hear the stories unfold. But in each story I've tried to be as faithful as possible to both the spirit and intent of the biblical record.

You may be surprised by the Jesus you meet in these pages. For Jesus is bolder and meeker, kinder and fiercer, more joyful and daring and puzzling than most of us have ever been taught.

Jesus knew that the best way to teach people the truth was to wrap it up in a story. My hope is that as you read these stories, you'll discover the truth for yourself. The truth about Jesus. The truth about the Mystery.

But be warned: Meeting the Mystery is never safe. This book may show you more of yourself than you really want to see. Because as Jesus reveals himself to you, he'll also help you see yourself more clearly. When he meets you, he redefines you.

And there's no turning back. Once you've been shown the truth that lies at the heart of the Mystery, once you've met him for yourself, you'll never be the same again.

God with us
CHAPTER ONE

(Matthew 1:18-2:23; Luke 1:26-56)

"Wake up!" His mouth is against my ear; his words urgent, rushed. Gently but firmly, he grabs my shoulder and shakes me awake. For a moment the strength in his hands startles me.

"What? What's wrong?" I open my eyes, but I'm afraid to move. My heart is thumping.

He pulls the warm wool blanket off me. A rush of cold air sends shivers down my spine. The flickering oil lamp in the corner of the room sends wild shadows dancing across the walls.

Joe is already dressed. "C'mon, we need to get outta here. Grab the baby and let's go."

"But it's the middle of the nigh—"

"I know what time it is. The longer we stay, the more danger we're in."

Now I'm really scared. The baby! My baby is in danger!

I stand up stiffly and rush toward the child. "How do you know?"

"Um . . . I'll explain on the way."

Wrapped up in thick blankets, sleeping in the cradle that Joe made for him, the baby looks so peaceful. So innocent. I pick him up gently. Even though Joe isn't the father, he has always looked out for him. Protected him.

As I glance around in the faint light, I notice Joe has grabbed only one small bag.

"Where are we going?"

"Far away. To Egypt," he says.

Egypt? I clutch the baby to my chest as Joe snatches up a few of his tools and the gifts we'd been given earlier that night and tosses them into the sack. Sure, the presents are valuable, but they'll hardly cover a trip to Egypt and back.

Or maybe we aren't coming back.

"We'll be safe. Hurry!"

Safe from what? I think, as he grabs my hand, and we stumble out into the chilly night. All I can think of is how I got into this predicament in the first place.

I never suspected I was pregnant.

The day I got the news I was totally surprised. Shocked. This pregnancy was about as unplanned as they come.

Not only was I surprised, I was also scared. I had so many questions. *What do I do now? Who could I talk to? Who could I trust?*

I kept thinking, *I'm 14 years old, I've never even kissed a guy, and I'm gonna have a baby!*

I could just hear people talking. "Another pregnant teen. Another unwed mother. Just what we need. What is this country coming to?"

But I am married! Well, sorta. Joe and I had been engaged for a couple of years, since I was about 12. Yeah, I'll admit it's a little young, but he was a good guy with a steady construction job. And he loved me.

But I knew how my friends would react to the news. Whispers. Rumors. Getting all quiet when I walked by. Stepping aside to let me pass. Talking about me when I wasn't around. I knew the names they'd call me, the things they'd say. Who could blame them?

Where could I turn? I'd never felt so alone.

For starters, pregnant teens aren't exactly welcome in my town. Usually, they'd do their best to keep it quiet for as long as possible and then, when word leaked out, there'd be trouble. Big trouble.

When I was just a kid, there was this girl who was caught in bed with her boyfriend. Her relatives didn't waste any time with lawyers or lawsuits. They just gathered some neighbors, formed a little mob, dragged her into the street, and killed her. Premarital sex is not taken lightly here.

I wondered how soon it would be until the neighbors found out about me.

No one was gonna believe my story. Everyone would think Joe and I had slept together. And since he's 31, we'd both be in trouble. Everyone would blame him for taking advantage of me, saying he should have known better, that it was his fault. Then the law would get involved—and who knows what would happen.

But the thing is, Joe and I had never had sex. Honest! Our relationship wasn't physical at all. Oh, I know what you're thinking now. "She's engaged to this one guy, and there she is sleeping around!"

But I wasn't! I swear!

It was all so confusing. I wished there was an easy way out—or at least someone to talk to.

I guess I could've told Joe. "Hi, sweetie, how was your day? Things have been a little slow here. By the way, Gabe stopped by. Yeah, the angel who appeared to Daniel about 600 years ago. He told me I'm gonna have God's baby even though I'm still a virgin. My son is gonna be King of the Universe. Other than that it's been a pretty boring afternoon." What would he think? What would you think—that I'd been eating rotten figs again?

All he had to do was say the word, and I'd be killed.

Now don't get me wrong. Joe is a really strong believer. I didn't think he'd turn me in, but honestly, I couldn't expect him to stick with me either. After all, it's not his baby. He'd be ridiculed, mocked. Maybe worse. And the angel hadn't even mentioned him. So I assumed I'd be a single parent, going it alone.

Even if Joe believed me, who else would? Sure we could rush and get married. But it doesn't take that much effort to count the months. Everyone would be thinking we were sleeping together before we got married, or at least there'd always be questions about who the father really was. If our engagement did survive, it would ruin Joe's career. We'd be outcasts forever. Despised. Alone.

So I just stood there pinching myself, thinking, *Okay, Mary, chill out. That was a real angel. You are not imagining things. You are not crazy. You are not crazy.*

But who would believe me? I just wished there was someone I could talk to. Someone who could understand how a girl feels when—

Liz!

The angel had said something about my cousin Liz being pregnant as well. She and her husband had been trying for years to have kids. I kept wondering why God hadn't answered their prayers and given them a child. But now! What had the angel said? "Nothing is impossible with God!"

I had to be sure. And I had to talk to someone who would be able to understand. So I grabbed a few things and headed to Liz's place in the country.

The trip took me about a week, which was pretty good time, considering. I mean, a young girl traveling the streets by herself? You know the kind of stuff that can happen. But I guess God was with me—no, I know he was. I arrived safe and sound.

And then I knocked on her door.

"Hello? Anyone home?" The door was unlocked, so I walked in. "Liz, you are not gonna believe what happened to me last week!"

"Mary? Is that you?"

You should have seen her face when I walked into the room.

The second she saw me, she started calling me God's mommy and stuff like that, really honoring me. She even said that the baby she was carrying jumped for joy when I walked in the door. It blew me away.

That was it. That moment I knew for sure everything was for real. I couldn't keep it in anymore. I just burst out singing!

I stayed to help during her pregnancy. And then after Liz had her baby (it was a boy, by the way), I knew I needed to return to Nazareth. I had to tell Joe. Regardless of how he might respond, he had to know. And I wanted to be the one to tell him.

I mean, think about it. One day I'm there, and the next I'm gone. No word. Nothing. Then three months later I return home—three months pregnant. I wanted to make sure I caught up with him before the rumors did.

I went straight to the construction site. When he saw me, he threw down the saw and came jogging over to me, calling out, "Mary, where have you been? I heard . . ."

He knew.

Maybe it was the look on my face. Or the way I stood. Or the stories he'd heard. But somehow he knew.

"Joe, let me explain."

"Are you . . . ?"

I told him. And as I did, he lowered his eyes. I rambled on about God and angels and miracle babies, kings and thrones and impossible promises.

And then he looked at me. It wasn't sadness in his eyes—or even disappointment, like I'd expected. He didn't seem angry, just sort of confused. I knew he was trying to believe me, to piece it all together. He wanted me to be telling the truth, but a storm of emotions passed over his face.

"It's true, Joe. It's a miracle!"

"Mary, I need to think." Then he turned and walked away.

I couldn't blame him. After all, I'd needed three months to let the news sink in. I couldn't expect him to be jumping off the walls the moment I arrived back home. But watching him walk away that day was one of the hardest things I'd ever done. Would he come back? Or would I be facing the future alone? A voice inside of me was screaming, *No! Come back! I'll do anything you want—just don't walk away from me!*

That night I begged God to show Joe the truth, to make it clear to him.

That's when I started thinking about the name the angel had told me to give my son. You'd spell it "Jesus" or Joshua. But of course we spelled it "Yeshua," like the warrior who replaced Moses as the leader of our people and like the high priest during the time when they rebuilt our temple. The angel said he'd be a king! My son, the Warrior, the Priest, the King!

His name means, "Yahweh saves." Yahweh! God's name, the name he told to Moses. It means, "I AM." Or as my father told me when I was growing up, "The One who is always present." I was carrying Yeshua—"the God who is always present, the God who saves." Hadn't Isaiah the prophet written that when the Messiah came, he would be called "Immanuel," that is, "God with us"? It was true!

God with us . . .

The angel had said I'd be with child. How strange—when it's really the other way around. The child would be with me.

———————

As we grab the donkey to saddle her for the journey, Joe turns to me.

"Don't be afraid, Mary. Our God will be with us."

Our God will be with us . . . just as he was with Moses and Joshua and Daniel and Isaiah. Our God will be with us—the promise whispered through the centuries ever since the days of the prophets. Most people don't believe in that stuff anymore.

But I do. As I look down into little Yeshua's eyes, I realize God is already with us: to go anywhere we go, to face any troubles we face, to calm any fears we have. So we never have to be alone again. Not ever.

And as I climb onto the donkey and prepare for the trip, the child reaches out his hand for me. And smiles.

making it personal

"I am the Lord's servant," Mary answered.
"May it be to me as you have said." Then the angel left her.
—Luke 1:38

As much as Mary trusted, as spiritual as she was, as faithful as she was, as "full of grace" as she was, she still had questions. She couldn't help it. That angel's promises just weren't logical. They didn't make sense. How could God be born? How could the One who shaped the universe let himself be shaped in her womb? How could her helpless child be the Almighty God? God with a bellybutton?! It was the greatest mystery and the wildest joke ever told. And it was being told through her life.

And there were consequences in trusting that angel. It would mean a different life from that moment on. People would talk. People would shake their heads. They might not believe her ever again. She'd be rejected. Alone. Forgotten and despised.

But she said "yes," despite the questions. She said "yes," because she had faith.

So she became the mother of the Mystery. And she pondered it all in her heart (Luke 2:19), treasuring it all up but never fully understanding it. From the moment she placed her child in that manger to the day she saw him hang on a cross, Mary lived with the most indescribable and irresistible mystery of all. And of course, the questions that came with it. With him.

And she found the wonder and joy of seeing God in the flesh. Of teaching him right from wrong. Of protecting him from danger. She watched the unchangeable change. She held hands with the Almighty. She rocked to sleep the One who never slumbers.

Try filtering all that through your typical Sunday school lesson! Try telling that to your friendly neighborhood churchgoer! It doesn't make sense. It's not supposed to make sense.

Loving your enemy doesn't make sense. Laying down your life for people who hate you doesn't make sense. But a God we can understand and figure out and put into our little box of reason would have to be a pretty small god indeed.

And so the child grew. And he learned to love Mary in a mysterious way—as his sister through faith and his mother through birth. The paradox of all paradoxes—she was both the mother of God and the child of her Son.

She trusted but didn't understand. She carried the Mystery inside her. She raised him. She changed his dirty diapers. She's an example for us all of the courage and the foolishness and the boldness and the wonder of faith.

So even today she is the sister of all who believe. And her Son is still with us. Still in us. Still reaching out his hand for us. And smiling.

Especially in that life-changing moment when we finally believe.

taking it deeper

1. Think of what it was like for Mary to say "yes" to that angel. Why might she have hesitated? If you were Mary, what would you have said?

2. What does it tell you about Mary's faith that she said "yes" right away? What lessons can we learn from her?

3. Mary said "yes" to the mystery of God's presence in her life—and her life was changed forever. How has God's presence changed your life? In which areas do you see the most change? Where do you see the least change? What will you do about that?

4. Mary had some questions for the angel. What questions keep you from drawing closer to Jesus? Did Mary's questions get in the way of her faith? What can you learn from that?

5. Is there a difference between knowledge and faith? How would you describe that difference to an alien from another planet? (Hint: Check out Hebrews 11:1 for a quick definition of faith.)

6. Did Mary need more knowledge or more faith? What about you?

7. Some people describe Mary as "full of grace." What do you think they mean by that? Read Ephesians 2:8-9. Could that phrase be used to describe your life, too?

8. In Matthew 28:20 Jesus makes an astonishing promise to his friends. Look it up. How does this verse relate to the story? How does it relate to your life today?

9. Do you live as if this verse is true? What difference would it make in your life if you were to trust Jesus' promise that he will always be with you? How would that affect the way you pray? The way you handle problems? The times you feel lonely? What changes will you make in your life based on this verse?

God with us

breaking free

Jesus,
you were with mary.
you were with joseph.
and you're with me, too.
you are the One who is always present.
    you are the One who saves.
help me to have the same kind of faith that mary had.
sometimes i'm not sure
what to think or what to believe.
sometimes my questions
get in the way. help me to remember
that your plan for my life is bigger
than my grandest dreams . . .
your love is greater than my sin . . .
and your grace is greater than my past.
    help me to say, "i am your servant,
may it be to me as you have said."
you're a mystery to be sure.
but a mystery i want to be a part of.

help me to believe—really believe—
and then to live out that faith.
amen.

alone in the boat
CHAPTER TWO

(Matthew 4:18-22)

It was a bright morning. Cool. A little breezy. Wind scurried across the lake and snatched at my hair.

My sons and I had spent the night fishing, out on the boat. And just like so many other times, we'd come home, taken our fish to the market, and returned to the boat to mend the nets for the next night. Since they were teenagers, they liked the staying up late part, but they always grumbled about the mending the nets part. Eh, who could blame 'em?

I don't remember exactly what we were talking about—the weather, maybe, or the fishing. I remember telling them I didn't have many years left to be taking them out like this. Soon the boat and the business would all be theirs.

It's a good life. Predictable. Steady. Good income. Sensible. I'd told them stuff like that before.

And that's when we saw him.

He was walking along the shore, a few other fishermen with him. We'd heard of this man—a real troublemaker. His name was Jesus. I recognized the two men with him: Peter and his brother Andrew. We'd fished together lots of times. They own a boat just up the shore from us, and they're good friends of my boys James and John.

I glanced toward their boat. Empty.

What were they doing with this man? Where were they going when there was so much work to be done? I set down the net for a moment and stared at them.

He'd been a carpenter, I guess. That's what people said. But then one day he just took to the streets to travel and preach. They say he tells a lot of stories, wastes a lot of time.

He was gesturing wildly with his hands. I couldn't quite make out what he was saying, but it must have been funny, because the men with him were all laughing.

Then he called to us, "Come here!" His voice cut through the sound of the morning breeze. "Come on! Follow me!"

Was this guy serious? He waved his hand for us to join him. Follow him? Where? Toward what?

"I'll show you how to fish for people!" he says.

Fish for people?! And the men with him just nodded and smiled. Peter made fish lips at us, and Andrew broke into laughter.

What had gotten into them?

What kind of a lunatic is this? How do you fish for people?

He hadn't stopped walking. "Come on!" he called again. In a moment he would pass us by.

I just shook my head and went back to work. You can't just drop everything and follow someone like that. It's not how the world works.

But then, to my amazement, I heard James whisper,

"What do you say, guys? Dad? John? Let's go. Let's do it."

Before I could say anything, I heard the sound of sandals landing on the wet sand as James and then John jumped from the boat. Together they headed up the shoreline toward this man.

"Hey! Where are you going?!" I yelled. "There's work to be done! What do you think you're doing? We need to finish fixing these nets!" The wind blew hard against my back, whistling in my ears.

For a moment they hesitated, and I thought they might just give up this nonsense. Then James turned and motioned for me to join him. "C'mon, Dad!" he yelled. "C'mon!"

And that's when Jesus looked at me. The sunlight glinted in his eyes. He tilted his head and gestured toward me as if he were inviting me to come, too.

Yeah, right. As if I was gonna follow *him*!

I just stood there yelling to my sons. "What are you doing? We have nets to mend! We have work to do! We have to make a living here!" Anger churned inside me. I could feel my chest rise and fall, rise and fall. Like the waves. Like the ocean. My sons weren't coming back. They were walking away from me, from everything I'd worked for! I almost ran from the boat to grab them, to drag them back. To end this foolishness right then and there.

"You don't even know this man!" I shouted.

But then another thought caught hold of me. *No, let 'em go, Zebedee! If they wanna walk away from all this, let 'em. If they wanna walk away from their own father, let 'em. They'll probably come crawling back in a few weeks anyway. After they find out that fishing for people doesn't pay all that well. And that you can't fry up and eat what you catch.*

"Fine, then!" I screamed after them. "Go on! Leave me! But I'm staying right here. Do you hear me?! I'm staying right here!"

There comes a time in your life when you gotta decide what you're gonna live for. Who you're gonna follow. They could follow this Jesus character if they wanted to. Let 'em. I made my choice that day, too.

I stayed right where I was, like any sensible person would have done.

For a few moments I stood there in silence with the wind tugging at my hair, watching as my two sons walked away. For a while

alone in the boat

their footprints glistened in the morning sun. Then the waves washed over them, and they blurred together, disappearing into the sand.

Then I cursed him under my breath and went back to work, fixing my nets.

making it personal

> Going on from there, he [Jesus] saw two other brothers, James son of Zebedee and his brother John. They were in a boat with their father Zebedee, preparing their nets. Jesus called them, and immediately they left the boat and their father and followed him.
>
> —Matthew 4:21-22

Don't miss those three telling words in that last sentence: "and their father." They're easy to skip over, but they say so much.

Sure, James and John left the boat to follow Jesus. They left their careers, their possessions, their priorities, their dreams—all that was involved in leaving the boat. But they also left their dad. Why?

Because he wouldn't come. He heard the call of Jesus just as they did. He heard the words, and he didn't follow.

He stayed in the boat that day.

The time had come for them to make a choice. Who would they follow with their lives? The boys chose Jesus. Their father did not.

The Bible records more than a dozen instances when Jesus invited people to follow him. Sometimes they did. Sometimes they didn't. All too often they stayed right where they were. Because it's so secure there in the boat: so safe, so comfortable, so familiar. It's so easy to stay behind and watch Jesus walk away, out of your life.

Even though James and John are referred to throughout the Bible as "the sons of Zebedee," their dad never appears in Scripture again. We only see him this one time, sitting in the boat, watching his sons walk away. That's his legacy.

Their mom appears, though. She's the sly, power-hungry schemer who tries to convince Jesus to make James and John the first and second in command of his kingdom (check out Matthew 20:20-28). That's her legacy.

Each of these four people had to make a choice—the same choice every one of us has to make. What are we gonna live for? Who are we gonna follow? The boys chose Jesus. Their parents? Well, as far as we can tell, they chose something else.

When Jesus walked on this earth, only a few people followed him. Only a few still do.

taking it deeper

1. What do you think it means to be a follower of Jesus today? How can we follow him when he's no longer visibly here? (Hint: See Matthew 28:19-20.)

2. Think of a time when you heard Jesus' voice loud and clear. What did you do? Did you step out of the boat or not? What will you do now?

3. When we follow Jesus, he doesn't promise a comfortable journey. Instead he hands us a cross and says, "Follow me . . ." Read Luke 14:25-35. How is Jesus' description of Christianity different from what you may have heard? What difference will that make in your life?

4. Is Christianity mainly a set of beliefs or a new way of life? Is it mainly a philosophy or a lifestyle? What's the difference? Based on that distinction, can you say you are a follower of Jesus? Why or why not?

5. Following Jesus always means leaving something behind. What is Jesus asking you to leave behind? What things don't belong in your life? What do you need to walk away from in order to follow him?

6. Read Hebrews 12:1-2. What two things do these verses tell you to do as you follow Jesus? Will you do them?

alone in the boat

7. Following Jesus often means leaving someone behind, because not everyone who hears his voice chooses to follow him. Do you know someone who has refused to follow him? What can you do for that person to show him or her the lasting benefits of following Jesus?

8. James and John left their old lives and followed Jesus toward a new life of danger, uncertainty, faith, and mystery. It meant walking away from a secure life with the people they loved the most. What new shore is Jesus calling you toward? Will you go, even if those closest to you choose to remain behind?

9. Read Galatians 5:25. What changes do you think God wants you to make to walk more closely in step with Jesus?

breaking free

okay, Jesus, here's the thing—
i've heard your voice . . .
i've heard you say, "follow me!"
and . . .

> *well . . .*
> *i've hesitated . . .*

i've held back,
or at least i've held back parts of myself.
i've looked around and wondered
if i might not be better off where i am
than following you. 'cause it seems so safe here.
so easy. so comfortable.

my soul needs a jumpstart from your Spirit.
shake me loose from the status quo
give me the guts to follow you—
wherever that might lead.

i want to leave the boat. i want to walk with you.
show me how to do that right now,
in this moment.
amen.

eavesdropping in the desert
CHAPTER THREE

(Luke 4:1-13)

A lone figure, gaunt and gasping, leans against a rock in the barren wilderness. A scorpion scuttles across the parched earth nearby. High above, the sun rages in the cloudless sky. And then a snake appears, wispy and writhing, at the man's feet. It is the color of midnight, and words slowly drip from its fangs . . .

S-s-s-s-s-o, just look at you, my old friend. Just look at you. My, my, my.

With that tight suit of skin stretched across your meat . . . Eyeballs to limit your vision . . . Stuck in time . . . Stuck in place . . . How does it feel to be so . . . um, confined? So temporal? So dependent?

Decay, Jesus. That's what you chose. Death and decay. The moment you entered the food chain, that's what you chose. Sweat. Tears. Blood. And decay.

Oh, I remember the times we shared so long ago. Back in the early days before you could bleed. Good times they were, back in the prelude to the world. Just you and I laughing with the angels at the dawn of time.

And then . . . well, you know the story. I was a bit ambitious back then. I admit it. But what can I say? You can't fault me for wanting a little piece of the pie. It's a big pie, after all, and I only wanted a slice or two.

And so here we are. But let's let bygones be bygones, shall we? Move on, as it were . . .

So where was I? . . . Oh, yes. Skin . . . decay . . . food chain . . . this dependence of yours on air and water and a beating heart. This choice of yours to become mortal and . . . vulnerable.

And hungry. Let's not forget your hunger. But what else could you expect? After all, how long have you been out here without any food—five, six weeks? It makes no sense to me, my friend. You take on the pathetic—excuse me, *fragile*—form of a human being (an animal that you yourself designed to need food, I might add), and then you deprive yourself of the very thing you need to survive . . .

And why? What are you trying to prove? Is this some kind of macho thing before entering the ministry? Is it political? Or religious maybe? A hunger strike for God? Or maybe it's for a woman? Be honest, now. Is there a woman involved—a set of pretty little eyes you're trying to impress? Oh, mister big, strong, tough Jesus?

I mean, you dress yourself in flesh and you're gonna have to face the consequences. Hunger. Thirst. Blisters. Heartache. Pain. They come with the territory, don't they?

And I know this is not a quiet hunger, Jesus. I can see it. I can smell it on your ragged breath. It's a desperate hunger, a deep and final hunger. And you're weak. Who wouldn't be? You're aching for food. Oh, my friend, I understand. Believe me. Hunger is the one human desire I truly understand.

C'mon, you've got the ability to take care of yourself, don't you? It's not wrong to provide yourself with something to eat. How could it possibly be wrong to do what you're designed to do? You have to eat or you'll die! It's the nature of the beast. Honestly, I can't stand to see you like this. We can have good times together again.

Go on. Turn some of those stones over there into bread. Do one of those little tricks of yours. What could be so bad about that?

Okay. You're right. Let's cut the crap here, save both of us some time. Here's the deal. You and I would make a good team. With my ambition and your powers, nothing could stop us. Not even your dad.

Hmm. I guess that sounds a little trite now that I say it, sorta like the villain in a superhero movie trying to lure the good guy over to his side. "Join me, Rabbi Man! Together we can rule the world! (Evil laugh. Evil laugh. Evil laugh. Evil laugh!)"

But here's the deal: I can offer you something your father never could.

Freedom.

Haven't you ever wondered what it would be like to have a little corner of the universe to yourself, to do your own thing? Just to do what you want for a change, instead of always having to do *his* will, carry out *his* plan, do *his* bidding?

I mean, why does it always have to be about him and his glory? Don't you deserve at least a little bit of the credit? Some of the reward? Haven't you ever wanted a little piece of the pie for yourself?

I mean, you love to talk about freedom, but you're not free at all. Not really. You're enslaved! There's nothing free about having to do what someone else tells you all the time. That's the opposite of freedom. The exact opposite.

Me, on the other hand, I have feasted on true freedom! I have let its juices run across my tongue! Oh, yes, I have known it. Complete and rich and succulent. And I'm telling you, there's nothing sweeter than the freedom to indulge in anything you choose.

Oh, my friend, you have no idea how it feels to be out from under the thumb of that ruthless dictator you call your father! Look around you. All of this is mine. Look beyond the horizon and see. See that—all the riches I possess? All the pleasures I control? They're mine. I'm the prince of this world. You know that. This is my domain. I own the keys to this side of the fence. And I am the keeper of all of this world's most succulent pleasures.

Freedom—true freedom—is never found in the place of rules and restrictions: Do this, don't do that; go here, don't go there; think this, don't think that. All those laws and regulations restrict freedom; they don't facilitate it. Real freedom isn't found in mindless servitude but in self-determination. Freedom is the exercise of the will, Jesus, not the denial of it.

You know what you want, my friend. What your body hungers for even more than food . . . What men fantasize about . . . Well, I can give it to you. All that your father forbids, I can supply . . . All that he denies you, I will provide.

C'mon, haven't you ever peered over the fence into the forbidden territory and wondered, just for a moment, what it would be like to taste the fruit he told you not to eat?

It can all be yours. All the pleasures that pitiful human body of yours can stand.

Think about it. What does your daddy offer you? Enslavement and pain. A life of sorrow and suffering, of crosses and thorns, of beatings and betrayals.

And what do I offer? Freedom and pleasure. Comfort and convenience. Gratification of all your desires. The freedom to indulge yourself.

Join me. A handshake between friends would do. Or better yet, give me a little bit of what you give him. If you do, I'll give you everything. All I ask for is a moment of your allegiance, not a lifetime. Not an eternity. All I ask for is a semblance of your love, not the real thing. All I ask for is the gesture of worship, not the heart that goes with it.

I ask so little. I offer so much. Give me just one moment, and I promise you—I vow to you—I will fill your mouth forever with all the sweet juices your father has forbidden you to taste . . .

So it's turned into this—a Scripture-quoting contest? How pathetic. Oh, I'm shaking in my snakeskin boots!

Daddy says this. Daddy says that. Well, I can play that game, too. "My angels will uphold you." Doesn't he say that? "So that you won't bump your little foot against a stone." Isn't that what he says?

Well, it's easy to make promises like that, but it's quite another thing to keep them. He's so full of promises, isn't he? So full of words. But from where I sit, action would be a lot more convincing. Words don't carry a lot of weight in my book.

I mock his promises! I spit on his words! As long as they remain untested, I call them fantasies! Illusions! Wishful thinking!

A little proof is all I ask.

Prove that he's as powerful as he says. Prove that your faith in him is complete. Right here. Right now. Prove once and for all that your daddy tells the truth and then . . . then, I'll leave you alone and you can get back to starving yourself to death in peace. I promise.

Jump.

Here, from this ledge. Step out in faith and let him save you. Let's see if he will. Let's see if he can.

Let's see if you really believe.

Go on. Or are you afraid? Scared? Worried that your daddy won't save you? Or maybe, could it be, are you worried that he can't?

Well, then . . . I suppose we should call it a day, huh? I'll have my people get in touch with your people. Maybe we can do lunch sometime. Or supper.

I'll be seeing you, Jesus. Sooner or later. Probably sooner, I'd venture to say, probably sooner. This is not over. It's only beginning. I promise you that much. It's only just begun.

But I guess it's goodbye for now, my old friend.

Yes, Jesus. I guess it's goodbye. For now.

making it personal

When the devil had finished all this tempting, he left him until an opportune time.

—Luke 4:13

It's a mystery how Jesus, being God, could be tempted at all. After all, God can't do evil because he is the essence of good, and it's impossible for him to contradict himself. God cannot disobey his own nature.

And yet Jesus was a human being. A man. Flesh and blood. And humans are all too vulnerable to temptation. In fact, everyone who has ever lived has given in to sin eventually—except for Jesus.

Here's what we know. Jesus was tempted—for real. He didn't dance with temptation; he wrestled with it.

Dealing with temptation wasn't a game to him. It wasn't just a front to make him look more human. It was real. Saying no to temptation was Jesus' way of saying yes to God.

And because of that, Jesus can help us when we're tempted, too.

Jesus never joked around about the devil. He took him seriously. He wasn't intimidated by him or afraid of him, but he wasn't flippant about him either.

Jesus warned his followers to watch out for the snares of the devil (Luke 21:34-36), to pray that they wouldn't fall into sin (Matthew 26:41), and to be wary and careful so they wouldn't fall away (John 16:1). And Jesus' example and advice on dealing with temptation are just as relevant today as they were 2,000 years ago.

taking it deeper

1. Read about Jesus' desert temptation for yourself in Matthew 4:1-11, Mark 1:9-12, and Luke 4:1-13. Notice that each of the writers emphasizes different things. What differences do you notice between the three accounts?

2. Matthew records a different order of the temptations than Luke does. Why? Does it matter? Why or why not?

3. According to Mark and Luke, how often during the 40 days was Jesus tempted? According to all three writers, who led Jesus into the desert? Why do you think that is?

4. What would have been so bad about Jesus turning the stones into bread? Think about it. Look at his responses to the temptations to see what would have been wrong about each of them. What was the purpose of his being in the wilderness in the first place?

5. What weapon did Jesus use against the temptations of the devil—logic, feelings, or truth? When he was tempted, did Jesus negotiate with the devil? What does this teach you about dealing with temptation in your life?

6. Read Hebrews 4:15-16. What qualifications does Jesus have to help you when you're tempted? According to these verses, can you have confidence when you pray for God's help?

7. Read John 8:44-45. According to Jesus, those who don't follow the truth belong to whom? At one time Jesus said that those on the side of truth listen to him (John 18:37). Who do you listen to? Whose side are you on?

8. When you're tempted, do you typically resist or give in? What does James 4:7 say will happen when you resist temptations that come your way?

9. Read James 1:13-15. When sinful desires get played out, what's the natural result? What will you do to combat them in your life? (See Ephesians 6:10-18.)

breaking free

God, i know what it's like to be tempted.
i know that all too well.
i know what it's like to see the glistening juices
of the forbidden fruit,
and to ease closer and closer until . . .
i bite down
only to find my mouth full of poison once again.

help me resist!
help me to obey you rather than the desires rising
from the dark parts of my heart!
my spirit is willing. my body is weak.
i admit it.
help me. give me the guts to say "no"
and the guts to say "yes"
and the wisdom to know when to
say which word.
amen.

night and day
CHAPTER FOUR

(John 3:1-21)

I can hear crickets jabbering in the shadows among the trees. Nearby in a clearing a campfire flickers. Jesus and his buddies are talking around the fire. I see them seated there in the dance of darkness and light. Someone laughs. Someone in the shadows coughs.

I've chosen to come at night when no one else can see me. No one else will even know I was here.

But I had to come. I had to meet him for myself. You see, I've heard him speak. I've seen his miracles. He's different. I know that much. There's something mysterious about him, yet something familiar, too—something that's both comforting and deeply unsettling.

I step on a twig, and it snaps underfoot. They all look up, silent now. I emerge from the shadows, and I'm sure they recognize by my clothes that I'm someone important, a teacher of the Jews. A couple of them smile and nod, obviously impressed that I would show up here to talk with their friend.

But before any of them can say a word, I clear my throat and address Jesus. "Rabbi," I say, bowing out of respect. "We know you are a teacher sent from God, for no one could possibly do the wonders you do unless God were with him."

I pause and wait for him to acknowledge the compliment.

But he doesn't say anything. He just studies my face. I can see the flicker of shadow and light on his features as the campfire leaps and twists a few feet away.

I expect him to say something like, "Gee, thanks. I appreciate that. So kind of you to mention it. Just trying to be faithful there. Just using the gifts and talents God has given me." But he doesn't, and that surprises me.

Instead he grunts, "So you think God's kingdom is proven by outward signs? Well, no one can even see God's kingdom unless he's born again."

Born again? What?

I try to wrap my mind around his words. *Is he trying to tell me I've never even seen God's kingdom? Does he know who he's talking to?!*

Everyone knows Jesus likes to use shocking images in his teaching, images of thieves and seeds and pigs and pearls, but . . . being born again? What's that supposed to mean?

My gaze drifts from Jesus to his disciples and then back to him. Finally, I say, "But how can that be, Jesus? How can someone be born again? You can't reenter the womb!" My words are alive with logic. I'm chuckling a little, but he isn't. Crickets chirp in the background.

"No one can enter God's kingdom unless he's born of water and the Spirit," answers Jesus, pushing a stick into the fire to reposition the coals. In the new light of the fire he must notice the bewildered look on my face because he motions for me to have a seat. I scrunch down on one of the logs they've pulled up beside the campfire. I see his wild features in the blazing light.

There's nothing tame about this man.

"We all know that humans have human babies. Well, God's Spirit produces spiritual babies." A cloud of sparks drifts skyward. "Your problem is that you think it's all explainable. But it's not supposed to be reasonable. The process is as mysterious as the wind. You can't even understand the direction of the wind—its origin or its destination. How can you expect to nail down spiritual birth? How are you gonna fit that into your neat little theological box?"

My heart is beating faster now. His words have an edge to them. He seems impatient with me, like he's talking to a child who hasn't been listening in school.

This guy doesn't beat around the bush, does he?

I watch the sparks rise into the darkness. They ride invisible currents of air, curling up into the night. Wind carries them along toward the stars—the wind of the fire, the breath of the flames. I watch them dance upward into the darkness and then disappear into the unknown. I'm trying to understand all that he's telling me. I really am. But I can't seem to make sense of it.

Finally, I shake my head. "I'm . . . I'm sorry. I don't understand."

And then Jesus loses his cool. He rises and steps toward me, filling the space between me and the fire. "You teach others, don't you? You teach the word of God . . . yet you don't understand it yourself?!"

I blink, unsure what to say. He sighs and shakes his head.

Then he speaks of purpose—the purpose of his life, the purpose of our lives, and the importance of faith at the center of it all. Over and over, in half a dozen ways, he tells me my problem isn't in my head, but in my heart. It isn't facts I need, he says, but faith. Not proof, but belief.

And he speaks to me of fear—the fear of being revealed. He tells me most people hide and are afraid to come into the light for fear that their evil deeds will be exposed.

Light and darkness . . . secrets and revelation . . . truth and lies . . . faith and fear . . . all of his words sail through my head.

He's saying I'm in love with the darkness! The words sting me. *That's what he's saying. That's what he means!*

The other men are silent. And then the truth hits me like a fist in the gut.

He's right, Nicodemus, you are afraid of the truth, you are in love with the darkness . . . Why else would you have come at night?

I swallow hard. How does he know? How can he see so deeply into my soul? How can he know my heart so well when we've only just met?

"But," he says at last, "whoever lives by the truth, Nicodemus, comes into the light."

His words don't sound like doctrine at all—more like an invitation.

Then Jesus is done. The fire crackles. There's nothing more to say. I nod to him. He nods back.

I look at the men sitting there, listening to all of this, studying me. I wonder how many of them have believed . . . have been reborn . . . have seen the kingdom . . . have stepped into the light.

Then I leave the fire and walk into the shadows again. And I wonder if I'm going into the shadows, or through them? Into or through . . .

His words snap at my heels as I stumble back home through the raven-black night.

Whoever lives by the truth comes into the light.

I notice stars flickering high above me like sparks from a thousand fires that finally found their way home through the night.

Am I walking into the night or through it to the other side?

"Through it," I say to myself. "I'm walking through it."

And I take a step forward.

Toward home.

making it personal

Later, Joseph of Arimathea asked Pilate for the body of Jesus.
Now Joseph was a disciple of Jesus, but secretly because he feared the
Jews. With Pilate's permission, he came and took the body away.
He was accompanied by Nicodemus, the man who earlier had visited
Jesus at night.

—John 19:38-39

It's ironic that Nicodemus, the man who came at night, buried the Light of the World.

Back when he first met the Mystery, Nicodemus had lots of knowledge about God. But something was missing. So Jesus had to show him the foolishness of reason and the true wisdom of faith.

God is not an algebra problem to be solved or a biology specimen to be dissected. He is the heartbeat of the universe. God is a lover to be accepted, a truth to be believed. Becoming a follower of Jesus means entering a riddle, not following a creed. It means stepping into a story, not agreeing with a doctrinal statement.

At first Nicodemus was trying to understand his way to faith, but he had it all backward. As St. Augustine wrote in his *Confessions*, "Seek not to understand so that you may believe, but believe so that you may understand." It all starts with faith.

You see, Nicodemus thought that the ways of God were logical and the power of God was predictable and sensible. But Jesus tore his fine-sounding arguments to shreds because they were based on what's seen instead of what's unseen. They were based on physical realities rather than spiritual realities.

Nicodemus thought of God's kingdom as external, visible, predictable, logical, natural, and based on evidence. Jesus showed him that it's *internal, invisible, unpredictable, mysterious, spiritual,* and based on *faith*. Nicodemus' view was upside down; his life was inside out.

So did Nicodemus ever become a true follower of Jesus, or did he simply remain an admirer? Did he walk to the edge of his understanding, step out of the darkness, and finally find his way home? It's hard to say. We're given clues, but we're not told.

Whether or not he did, we can. Sometimes we're tempted to be secret admirers of Jesus, to come to him only under cover of darkness. Yet only those who are honest enough to step into the light and stop hiding in the dark will ever truly be found.

Only they will find their way home.

taking it deeper

1. Read John 3:12-18. Count the number of times Jesus refers to faith or belief. Why did he emphasize it so much? What does it tell you about his priorities?

2. According to these verses, what is the key to receiving eternal life with God? What was getting in the way of Nicodemus receiving new life?

3. Obviously, Jesus wants us to believe in God. But is that all? Is that enough? Read James 2:19. What else does he want from you? What Bible verses support your view? How does John 5:39-40 relate to this story?

4. Read John 7:45-52. Why do you think Nicodemus stood up for Jesus? Do you think he was convinced that Jesus was innocent? Why do you say that?

5. It's easy to become intimidated by other people's opinions of us. Check out John 12:42-43. What reasons are listed for those people being secret followers of Jesus? What did Jesus have to say about people who want to follow him privately? (See Matthew 10:32-33 and Mark 8:38.)

6. John 19:39 tells us that Nicodemus brought the 75 pounds of spices used to preserve Jesus' body after he was crucified. What does that tell you about Nicodemus's commitment to Jesus? Do you think he remained simply a fan of Jesus, or did he become a genuine follower?

7. The greatest darkness in our lives is the one inside our souls, and the only way to let light in is to believe. Read 2 Corinthians 4:6. Who ignites the faith in our lives? So who gets the credit for our faith? How does that affect your pride?

8. In John 3:19-21 Jesus talks about darkness and light. Which does he say people prefer? Why is that? What areas of your life are currently cloaked in darkness? What will it take for you to expose them to the light?

9. What steps will you take to put John 3:21 into practice? When will you start?

breaking free

Breath of Life, breathe on me . . .
Wind of God, blow through me . . .
Spirit of Truth, rebirth me . . .
    pull back the covers of my practical, logical world
    and baptize my knowledge with the mystery of faith.
help me to believe and to stop trying to understand.
after all, how could i ever wrap my mind around something—
someone—
greater than the universe itself?

your presence doesn't make me comfortable,
    but it comforts me.
your light isn't easy to look at,
    but it reveals me.
the spiritual life is an absurd mystery.
help me to enter it,
as it enters me.
the first step isn't one of reason, but one of faith.
help me to take it. even now. even here. today.
amen.

the party animal
CHAPTER FIVE

(Matthew 9:9-13; Luke 15:11-32)

I threw a party. After all, I couldn't think of anything better to do.

I invited all my friends—all the other tax collectors and so-called "sinners." And let me tell you, we had a blast partying with Jesus. Good food. Wild dancing. Lotsa wine. For a religious guy, he sure knew how to party, I can tell you that much right now.

Actually, I don't think he'd really want me to call him religious. After all, he shied away from the word *religious*. Come to think of it . . . I can't remember him ever telling anyone to be more religious. Huh. That's kinda odd, don't you think? Considering who he was.

All the tax collectors and other so-called "sinners" were flocking to Jesus. He would party with them and dine at their homes. But the Pharisees and other religious teachers just shook their heads and muttered, "Look at this guy. He welcomes sinners and eats with them."

And so, Jesus told them this story . . .

The first time we met, I was at work, collecting taxes from the people. You see, it was my job to tally up what they owed the government and then make sure they paid it. My salary came from how much I could overcharge the people. That's how I got my paycheck—my big, fat paycheck.

Everyone knew we were cheating them. That's why no one trusted us tax collectors. Everyone hated us.

But hey—it's the way the system worked.

"Give me your money," I'd say. And they would hand it over.

A man had two sons. One day the younger son went to his dad and demanded his inheritance. "Look, Dad," he sneered. "Give me my money. I've got plans. I've got dreams. Why should I wait around here for you to die before I start living my life?"

And so the father figured out how much the boy would get upon his death. He withdrew the cash from the bank. And he handed it over.

I had a nice office overlooking the beach in the seaside city of Capernaum. So there I was, at work balancing the books and collecting the tax money, when he comes walking up to me with a whole crowd of people behind him.

"Follow me," he says.

That's it. Two words. A simple invitation to a new life. Almost too simple.

And you know what?

I accepted.

I just stood up and walked away from everything I'd ever known. I wanted to be as close to him as I could.

The boy walked away from everything he'd ever known. He wanted to be as far away from his family as he could. As soon as he'd packed up his things, he left for a distant land.

There he began to live the way he'd always dreamed. Indulging himself. Physically. Sexually. Whatever he wanted, he went after. He dove headfirst into the wild life and never even thought about home.

Until finally, he'd spent all he had, down to the last penny. Bad timing, too. Because right then, the bottom dropped out of the economy in that country.

The poor guy was out of money and out of luck. So he got the only job he could get—out on a farm, tossing slop to the pigs. It was pretty despicable.

I was pretty despicable.

So why did I follow him? Well, that's a good question.

I guess you could say I finally came to my senses.

One day he came to his senses.

"What am I doing here?" he said to himself. "Even these pigs have more to eat than I do. The guys my dad hires to work in his fields have plenty of food on the table, while I'm stuck here starving half to death! I oughta go back home, grovel a little, and see if my dad will hire me. I could earn back the money and pay him back!"

Jesus had saved me, and I could never pay him back. So how could I show my thanks? Well, the best way I could think of was to introduce him to my friends.

That's when I decided to go back home and throw a party. I invited all the guys from work, Jesus, his disciples, a whole bunch of other people.

The place was packed. I spared no expense.

When Jesus arrived, he ran over to greet me.

When the son arrived, his dad ran over to greet him. The son began his explanation, but the father stopped him midsentence.

"Quick!" he said to one of the workers. "Bring some new clothes for the boy—the best we have—and get rid of all these filthy, stinky rags. Kill the calf. Tonight we'll have prime rib, T-bones, and veal! My son is home! It's time to party!"

"I'm sorry," I tried to say. "For all the times I've cheated people. For all the . . . "

But Jesus stopped me midsentence.

"All that can wait," he said. "It's time to party!" He threw his arms around me and kissed me on the cheek, just like we'd been friends forever! Like I was a part of his family!

He wasn't ashamed to be seen with a tax collector.

He wasn't ashamed to be seen with a pig farmer. He threw his arms around his son and welcomed him home.

And so they began to celebrate. The music was loud; the dancing was wild—it was great. You could have heard it all the way across town.

And so we began to celebrate. The music was loud; the dancing was wild—it was great. You could have heard it all the way across town. And I guess some people did.

Because that's when the Pharisees arrived.

That's when the older brother arrived.

But they didn't want to join the party. They just stood outside and shook their heads.

He just stood outside and shook his head.

"Why are you throwing a party for him?" he said. "This son of yours wastes his money on prostitutes, and you throw him a party?! He's a worthless sinner!"

"Why does Jesus associate with them?" they said. "These people have cheated others out of their money, and he attends their party?! They're worthless sinners!"

"But don't you understand?" said Jesus. "I have to celebrate. These are the people I came for. Not the ones who think they're already fine, but those who know they're not!"

"But don't you understand?" said the father. "We had to celebrate. Your brother was dead and is alive again; he was lost and is finally found!"

Then the father went back to the party. And the older son just walked away.

Then Jesus came back to the party. And the Pharisees just walked away. It's too bad they wouldn't join our party. There was plenty of food and lots of room.

Oh, well. They probably wouldn't have fit in all too well here. After all, this is a party for sinners, not religious people. And as long as you think you're fine, you'll never feel at ease with Jesus—because you'll never realize you need him.

Yeah, this is one party you'll never be able to enjoy until you finally come to your senses.

making it personal

While Jesus was having dinner at Matthew's house, many tax collectors and "sinners" came and ate with him and his disciples. When the Pharisees saw this, they asked his disciples, "Why does your teacher eat with tax collectors and 'sinners'?"
—Matthew 9:10-11

I'm gonna let you in on one of the greatest secrets of all time: God is into parties, not religion.

At the core of God's being is a deep desire to find the lost and then party with the found. That's why Jesus came (Luke 19:10). God isn't a quiet, reserved, reverent, mumbling monk in heaven. God is a party animal.

The Old Testament is packed with parties and festivals in honor of God. And in the New Testament Jesus himself compares the kingdom of heaven to a party more than to anything else.

Nope, Jesus never said, "The Kingdom of God is like a church service that goes on and on forever and never stops." No way. He said, "God's kingdom is like a homecoming party, a wedding, a banquet, a feast, a Thanksgiving dinner with your friends and family!"

Heaven is gonna be more like a dance club than an organ recital. More like a pep rally than a lecture on theology.

How about that. The kingdom of heaven is a party with God.

This idea was too radical for the religious leaders of his day. They were more concerned about etiquette, manners, traditions, and religious rituals than about partying with Jesus. And that's why they missed out. Jesus was too much of a party animal for them to accept (Matthew 11:19) and yet too pure to find any fault in (Mark 14:55; John 8:46).

the party animal

According to Jesus, the truly spiritual life is one marked by freedom rather than compulsion (John 8:36), love rather than ritual (Mark 12:30-33), and peace rather than guilt (John 14:27). Jesus saves us from the dry, dusty duties of religion and frees us to cut loose and celebrate. And I'll tell you what: That's my kind of Savior.

taking it deeper

1. Do you tend to think of God as a party animal? If not, what is your image of God? Is your view of heaven more like Jesus' view or more like that of the Pharisees?

2. On several occasions Jesus compared himself to a groom (see Matthew 9:15 and 25:1-13). John the Baptist also called Jesus the groom (John 3:27-29), and in the book of Revelation the arrival of believers in heaven is symbolized by a marriage between the Lamb (Jesus) and his bride. (See Revelation 19:7 and 21:2, 9.) When Jesus started his public preaching ministry, what was the first thing he did after recruiting his followers and being baptized? (See John 2:1-11.) Why do you think he did that?

3. What does all Jesus' talk about weddings, parties, and homecomings tell you about heaven? Will it be fun, exciting, and adventurous or solemn, tedious, and boring? How should that knowledge of heaven change your view of following Jesus here on earth?

4. Read Luke 15. What complaint do the religious leaders have with Jesus? What answer does Jesus give them by means of his stories? In the last story, Jesus never revealed whether or not the older brother ever joined the party. Why do you think he left the story unfinished? Why is that significant?

5. Did Jesus care what the religious people thought of him? Did their opinion of him change the way he acted or the people he hung out with? What does that tell you about his priorities?

6. Where do you see yourself in Jesus' stories in Luke 15? With which character do you most identify? Where would you like to fit in? What will you do about that?

7. What type of attitude closes people off from partying with God in the kingdom of heaven? How has your attitude about Jesus changed as a result of studying this story?

breaking free

Jesus, Life of the Party,
i love your stories.
i see myself reflected in them.
your words are mirrors for my soul.

sometimes i'm the younger brother,
*   greedy and impatient,*
*   lost and alone,*
*   wandering far from home.*

sometimes i'm the older brother,
*   resentful and bitter,*
*   legalistic and judgmental,*
*   drifting into the traps of duty and performance.*

i'm walking toward you,
*   i'm drifting away.*
i'm returning home,
*   i'm running off.*
Jesus, i'm stuck somewhere between being lost
and being found.

show me my true self.
find me and bring me home to the great party
that looks a little like a kingdom
in disguise.
amen.

the cell
CHAPTER SIX

(Matthew 3:1-17; John 1:19-34; Matthew 11:2-11)

When I close my eyes, I can almost see the ripples rolling along the surface of the river . . . I can almost taste the wild honey melting on my tongue . . . I can almost smell the scent of wildflowers caught on the desert wind . . . I can almost remember my old life.

Almost.

But not quite.

And I can't keep my eyes closed forever.

So I open them and look around my cell. I can't see much in the musky darkness. No rivers here. No honey. And I don't even want to mention the kinds of smells there are in here. A few small shadows scurry into the corner. Rats. So that's what I felt crawling across my neck last night.

I sigh and close my eyes again.

Now I see bubbles rising through the water as a face emerges, floating up toward me. It's the face of a man . . . it's him . . . rising to the surface. My left hand supports his shoulders . . . and now he's standing on his own again, droplets of water glistening on his dark beard . . . He's smiling. Joy wraps its arms around this moment. The crowd is cheering. Even heaven itself seems to applaud, seems to shout his name.

This is my Son; he is the one! . . .

I hear the words deep within my heart.

He is the one . . .

A dove rests upon his shoulder.

He is the one!

And then the image fades, and it's a day earlier. I see the crowds gathering around me. They're asking me if I'm the one, the Christ. But I shake my head no.

"Are you the prophet?"

"No."

"Are you Elijah, then?" They pepper me with questions. Their faces blur together in my memory.

"No," I say. "I'm the voice calling in the wilderness. The one who is coming is the one you seek."

He's here . . . I hear the words. *It's him. He's the one . . .*

I can't keep quiet. "The Lamb of God!" I shout to them. "He's the Lamb of God who has come to take away the sin of the world!"

The Lamb of God!

That's what I told them. That's what I believed. I was so sure of myself. Back then. Before all this.

I open my eyes again. Darkness. Shivers. The smell of death.

My ankles are in chains, and so is my soul. I'm like a caged animal here in this cell. My soul aches to be in the open spaces again. To be free. And my heart aches, too. It aches for certainty. It aches to be sure again. To be confident. Full of faith. Not riddled with questions. Haunted with doubt here in my cell.

You see, after I baptized him, I expected things to change. And they did, a little. His disciples started baptizing people, too. And some of my followers left me to follow him. Andrew was the first to go. The ones that remained asked me about it. "He's the reason I came," I said. "He's the one. He's the Son of God. The one who is from above is above all. He who comes after me has surpassed me, because he was before me! And now that I have seen him, my joy is complete."

And so more left.

A few stayed, but most left.

And I told the rest that was good. That was the point. But now . . .

Well, I don't really know how to say this . . . I've started to wonder which of the images are memories and which ones are dreams.

The voice in my heart—was it real or not? The dove from above—was it simply a coincidence? The thunder from heaven—was it just the roar of the river, magnified by my excitement?

After he went his way, I wasn't really sure what to do. I kept baptizing and teaching and preaching. I kept speaking my mind. And that's what landed me in here—the king wasn't too happy when I told him he shouldn't be sleeping with his brother's wife. So he stuck me here. He locked me up—alone with my doubts.

And the one I was so sure of, well . . . I've heard more and more stories about him. Healings and miracles. They even say he can raise the dead. But I don't hear about him taking away the sin of the world. At least not yet. And he hasn't visited me. He hasn't even sent word. And so I've begun to wonder if I was right, if I really heard that voice, or if maybe it was all just wishful thinking . . .

Is Jesus really the Deliverer or just another person like me who needs delivering?

Ever since I was a little kid I've known I was put on this earth for a reason, a very specific purpose. I came to announce the coming of the kingdom, the arrival of the king. That was my calling. My task. My life. To be the voice.

"He must become greater," I said at one time. "And I must become less."

But now . . . well, life isn't turning out like I expected. I hear rumors of his power, but charlatans and tricksters are a dime a dozen. I want to know. I need to know if he really is the one. Can I stop waiting, stop searching? Or should I keep looking for the Messiah? Maybe the one isn't here yet. Maybe Jesus isn't the mighty savior I thought he was.

So that's why I sent two of my remaining followers to ask him the question. The question that matters most, the only question that matters at all: "Are you the one? Or should we wait for and believe in and follow someone else?"

They should be back anytime with the answer.

Until then I have nothing to do but think. And wait. I close my eyes and see his baptism again. Bubbles rising. Water glistening. Sunlight dancing. Laughter and shouting. Confidence and joy.

It all seems so far away.

My doubts rise again like those bubbles in the river. Is my faith still real? Can doubt and faith live together in the same heart at the same time? Can you believe and yet still wonder if you really do believe? That's how I feel—as if my faith is being swallowed by my doubts.

I can hear footsteps now—the footfalls of my friends, echoing in the corridor. So they're here. The time has come. What will they say? What news do they bring?

Their footsteps come closer. My wait is almost over.

I open my eyes and edge closer to the door of my cell with images of his smiling face still rippling through my mind.

Ready to emerge.

At last.

making it personal

When John heard in prison what Christ was doing, he sent his disciples to ask him, "Are you the one who was to come, or should we expect someone else?"

—Matthew 11:2-3

John the Baptist was a fearless man of God who wasn't even intimidated to correct the king. He was bold, fiery, and uncompromising. And yet in his prison cell his certainty evaporated. He began to wonder. He began to question. He began to doubt.

So he sent his followers to ask Jesus: Are you the one we should believe in? Are you the one we've been waiting for? *Are you the one?*

This great man of faith, whom Jesus called the greatest man to ever live (see Matthew 11:11), had his doubts.

And for me that's reassuring. Because sometimes doubts worm their way into my faith as well. There are times when I wonder if my faith is still real or if my doubts have eaten it away to nothing.

How do faith and doubt coexist? Where do they connect? It's a mystery.

But it's a reality. Sometimes we have glistening moments of unwavering faith, and sometimes we get mired in the quicksand of doubts. And sometimes both happen on the very same day!

"Are you the one?" we whisper in our dark moments. "Or should I wait for another?"

And his answer comes to reassure us.

Yes . . .

To enlighten us.

Yes . . .

To guide us through our doubts and back to himself.

Yes! I am the one. Stop searching. Stop waiting. And let me emerge in your life at last.

the cell

55

taking it deeper

1. Read the answer Jesus gave to John's followers when they asked him if he really was the one (Matthew 11:4-6). In his answer Jesus quoted Isaiah 61:1. Look it up in the Bible. Why do you think Jesus quoted an Old Testament prophet in his response rather than just saying, "Yes! I'm the one!"?

2. Why do you think Jesus chose to quote from Isaiah? What special significance does this prophet have for John the Baptist? (Hint: Read John 1:23 and Isaiah 40:3.)

3. Why do you think Jesus said that those who don't fall away because of him are blessed (Matthew 11:6)? Do you think this encouraged John? Why or why not?

4. How can the story of John help you during your times of doubt or discouragement? What insights does Matthew 12:20 offer into how Jesus treats people who are weak in faith?

5. How do you feel when God seems invisible or absent, or when his promises to you don't seem to come true? What do you do about that? What happens?

6. The truth of who God is and what he has done can help us navigate through times of doubt. In John 8:31-32 what does Jesus suggest we should do during those times?

7. Some people think John sent his disciples to Jesus for their sake, not his—that they were the doubters, not him. The Bible doesn't say either way. Given that John was in prison and the context (Luke 7:14-19), what do you think? Why do you say that?

8. God has promised us many things in Scripture. What (or who) is his reassurance that they will all come true? (Hint: See 2 Corinthians 1:20.) How confident of that can we be?

9. Check out Mark 9:14-27 (especially verse 24). Can you identify with this guy who believed but also doubted? Does that ever happen to you? When? What did this man ask Jesus to do about his doubts? Will you do the same?

breaking free

Lamb of God,
sometimes my convictions become clouded,
my hope fades away,
my patience gets tried,
and my joy disappears.

questions infect my faith.
i get lonely. i get frustrated. i get discouraged.
> *i drift into the prison of doubt*
> *and feel its chains on my neck.*
and sometimes i wonder if you truly are the one.

show me that the answer to my questions
> *is not a formula, but a process,*
> *not a philosophy, but an adventure.*

pierce this moment with your presence
and wed my wonder to your word.

then walk with me through my valleys
of doubt and despair.
when faith seems impossible to me,
> *remind me that you specialize in the impossible.*
> *show me that faith doesn't only come someday*
after all the doubts are gone,
but that faith is what takes my hand
and leads me through the darkness
every step of the way.
amen.

fragments

CHAPTER SEVEN

(Luke 7:36-50)

There's a certain way men look at you. You can tell right away what they want. Their eyes crawl all over you, feeling you from across the room, making you feel dirty and used. But he looked at me differently, like I was a work of art, not a piece of meat.

I noticed it the first day I heard him teaching, the first time I ever saw him. I was in the crowd, just another face in the crowd. But not to him. Our eyes met. He smiled at me; he didn't leer. He looked me right in the eyes and nodded at me like I was royalty.

"I didn't come to heal those who think they're fine," he was saying. "I came to help those who are broken and want to be fixed."

That's me, I thought. *Did he really come for people like me?*

Another time I heard him tell a story about a search for a lost sheep. I guess it had wandered from the fold. And when the shepherd found it, he didn't kick it or punish it; instead he carried it home on his shoulders and celebrated with his friends.

"I am the Good Shepherd," the teacher said. "I know my sheep, and they know me."

He had come for people like me. And he wasn't ashamed of it.

He was the only man to ever look at me that way. That deeply.

His name was Jesus.

I'd been to Simon's house before. I knew my way around. He was one of my . . . um . . . more regular clients. Usually, I'd arrive sometime near the end of the meal and go upstairs to the bedroom. There was a back door for me. Then I'd wait for him. I never had to wait long.

But this night I hadn't come to see Simon. I'd come to see Jesus.

The servants showed me in. They recognized me. They knew me.

I didn't even look at Simon and the others. I just dropped to my knees at the feet of Jesus. I broke my jar of perfume. I poured it on his feet. And I wept.

I couldn't help it. It was like something inside of me snapped. A cord that had bound me to the past, to my choices—to everything I'd become—broke in half.

I smashed the jar open. I wasn't saving any of it for myself. I let all the perfume spill on his feet. It was all for him.

And just like that jar of perfume, my soul broke open in front of him. I wanted to say, "See! I'm the one you were talking about! I'm the sick one who needs healing, the lost one who needs finding, the broken one who needs fixing! Here I am!"

I wanted to say that, to say something—anything—but nothing came out. I tried, but all I could do was cry. I guess sometimes tears are the only words you have left.

I used to tell myself that I was what I was because of necessity. But then one day I realized I was rich, and I was still a prostitute. No, I wasn't doing it for the money. I was doing it because that's what I was. That's what I'd become. A whore.

He was talking to Simon, telling him a story. I heard that much. But then he said the words "her sins," and I realized he was talking about me.

" . . . Her sins, Simon—and they are many—have been forgiven. And so, as you see, her love is great. But whoever has been forgiven little loves little."

He said my love was great. Jesus called me a lover, not a slut.

And I did love him—he was right. Not in a romantic or erotic sense but in a deeply personal way. The way that matters. You know the kind of love I mean. You know the difference. I loved Jesus like that.

He came to find people like me—the hurting, the lost, the broken. To forgive us. And I wept because I knew how much I needed to be forgiven. And so I loved him. I did.

Love. It's such a strange word for someone in my profession, such an uncommon word. Because when you use someone to get what you want, that's the opposite of love. And I know all about using people and being used.

But Jesus spoke of love.

I used men to get money; they used me to get sex. We used each other. And that's not love. Love is about giving, not getting; sacrificing, not taking. Love is about accepting someone in spite of who they are, not because of it. Even I knew that. When you use someone, even though you're trying to fill yourself up, you both become more empty. But when you love someone, even though you're emptying yourself out for them, you both become more full.

How does all that work? I don't know. But it happens. I know it does. Because when he spoke to me, as withered and raw as my soul was, it began to heal. His love filled me up.

Then he turned to me. He looked at me. He spoke to me.

"Your sins are forgiven," he said.

The dinner guests gasped, "Who does this guy think he is, claiming to forgive sins?!"

But I didn't care about them, and neither did he. We ignored them. This was between us. That's the way it is with love. You don't care what other people think or say about you. All you care about is the one you love. "Your faith has saved you," he said. "Go in peace."

My choices had turned me into something I was never meant to become, but the forgiveness of Jesus changed me into a lover. That night I felt like a bride, not a harlot.

I reached out to pick up the broken pieces of my perfume jar to clean up, but he pushed my hand away, shaking his head no.

He wanted me to leave the broken shards behind.

And so I did. I left them there.

I left all the broken pieces behind that night—there at the feet of Jesus.

making it personal

> Then Jesus said to her, "Your sins are forgiven."
> The other guests began to say among themselves,
> "Who is this who even forgives sins?" Jesus said to the woman,
> "Your faith has saved you; go in peace."
> —Luke 7:48-50

Jesus is in the business of transforming people, of giving fresh starts and new beginnings. That night Jesus saw love and faith in the heart of a lost sheep, and he offered her peace and forgiveness. He carried her home. And he offers the same to us when he sees love and faith arise unashamed in our hearts.

Admittedly, the interplay of faith and love is a bit of a mystery in this story. Did the woman love Jesus because she'd been forgiven (as Jesus' story seems to indicate)? Or was she forgiven because she loved Jesus (as his comments seem to imply)? Don't spend too much time trying to untangle the causes and effects. Jesus said what he did for a reason. And it wasn't to give a logical argument for where love comes from. Rather, Jesus wanted to show the connection between debts forgiven and love expressed.

The greater the cancelled debt, the greater the love.

By the way, we don't know the name of the woman in this story. Some say it was Mary of Magdala (otherwise known as Mary Magdalene, the woman out of whom Jesus cast seven demons), but we don't really know. All we know for sure is that this woman, whatever her name was, was deeply in love with Jesus.

And that night she left in peace.

Too often our love for Jesus dries up because we're too focused on ourselves, rather than on him. We forget the size of our debt. Yet if we're too interested in loving ourselves and looking at how good we've been (like Simon), we may miss the most important thing of all—the love and forgiveness of Jesus. For it's only offered to those who are willing to fall down at his feet and believe.

taking it deeper

1. Luke refers to the woman in this story as a "sinner." Some Bible scholars believe the Greek word Luke uses means "prostitute," while others contend that the meaning isn't that specific. Either way, we know Jesus said, "her sins were many." Was Simon a sinner, too? What does his attitude toward the woman reveal about himself?

2. Did Simon look down on Jesus because Jesus accepted this woman? Where do you see his attitude repeated today? Why didn't he receive forgiveness that night? What got in the way?

3. While the woman was weeping at his feet, Jesus took the time to tell a parable to Simon. Read it in Luke 7:40-43. What do the debts in Jesus' parable represent? Why do you think Jesus said that neither man could repay his debts? What does that tell you about your relationship with God?

4. How would you define love? How do you think God defines love? (See 1 Corinthians 13:4-8 for some ideas.)

5. Simon didn't show much love at all for Jesus. Why not? Why did the woman show so much love?

6. How did the woman show her love: by feelings, actions, or both? What does that tell you about how love should flow out of your life?

fragments

7. Loving Jesus is closely related to obeying him. Read John 15:9-14. What does Jesus say shows genuine love for him? Can you ever express love for Jesus by disobeying him? Explain what you mean. So what is disobedience really evidence of?

8. What steps do you need to take to show your love for God?

breaking free

Father, the chains of my choices rattle in my soul . . .
. . . break them.
Jesus, the pains of my past haunt my dreams . . .
. . . heal them.
Spirit, the guilt of my sins suffocates my joy . . .
. . . remove it.

all too often,
i'm quick to sneer like simon,
yet slow to weep like the woman.
i'm quick to judge, yet slow to confess.

show me my sin, that i might see your forgiveness!
reveal to me the real me.
unearth me, the deep parts of me,
show me how dark is the stain,
that i might see how deep is your love.
i want to fall in love with you,
but first,
i must fall out of love with myself.

break my pride to pieces
that i might leave it at your feet
and finally find
the peace and forgiveness i need.
amen.

the good life
CHAPTER EIGHT

(Mark 10:17-24)

I was at a funeral yesterday. Everyone was there—everyone who was anyone. Crying, shaking their heads, wailing, dabbing at their tears. Saying things like, "He was such a nice young man." "He had such a bright future ahead of him." "He never even saw it coming." It was all very touching.

Me? I didn't say anything. I was silent.

After all, I was the one lying in the casket.

————————

I used to think money could buy anything. And I lived like it, too. For me success was spelled with three Ps—power, prestige, and possessions. And by that definition, I was quite successful. My reputation was flawless. I was rich. I was in control. But still I wasn't fulfilled. I wasn't truly happy.

Even religion didn't help. Sure, I did what the church required. I attended services regularly and gave 10 percent of my income to charity. I even helped lead the singing. Ask anyone, and they'd tell you I was a pretty good person.

I didn't pad my business deals. I didn't use different standards for different people. I guess you could say I decided to do things God's way.

But I still felt empty.

Through it all I tried to be the same person I was in the dark as I was in the light. True character is when you live with integrity, not duplicity.

I'd seen too many hypocrites in my life. I didn't want to be a hypocrite.

Anyway, I guess people noticed. People in high places. Because opportunities came along, and while I was still a young man, I was promoted to be the ruler of a certain region of our country.

And I felt pretty good about myself. I mean, I didn't smoke or drink or sleep around. I didn't lie or cheat or steal. I wasn't into drugs. And I had big plans for my life.

Now I'm not telling you all this to pat myself on the back or anything—don't misunderstand. I'm just telling you so you know where I was at, what was going on in my life.

But questions nagged me. You know, spiritual things. Questions about heaven and stuff like that.

I'd done my best. I'd done better than most people. But still I wanted to be sure I'd make it, you know? I wanted to sort of nail that down.

So when I heard about the Teacher, I went to see him. People said he had all the right answers—that he spoke the truth and he lived it, too. People said that he'd come from God—from heaven itself. I wasn't so sure about that, but I figured if anyone would know the answers to my questions, he would.

So one day when he was talking about prayer, I sat in and listened. He sure had some bizarre ways of teaching.

He told a story about these two guys who went to pray. One was a model citizen, and the other was, well, a cheat. A swindler. A real loser. And the righteous guy had every right to pray like he did, thanking God that he hadn't drifted into any shady business deals or illegal schemes or illicit affairs. And he thanked God that he was able to tithe. Just like me. In fact, he reminded me an awful lot of . . . me.

And all the while, the crook just knelt in the corner and begged God to forgive him.

So then Jesus wraps up his story by saying that only one of them went home forgiven and at peace with God. And who do you think it was? The guy who followed the rules and was a pillar of the community, or the swindler who just happened to have a change of heart that day? Yeah, you guessed it. The second guy. The tax collector. Because Jesus said he'd humbled himself before God.

See, like I said—bizarre. His stories had a way of getting your attention.

So anyway, I went up to him. Actually, I ran up to him and threw myself down on the ground, bowing low just like that tax collector in his story. I figured it would be a good way to show him I'd been listening. "Good teacher!" I said, "What should I do to get eternal life with God?"

And you know what he says?

"Why do you call me good? God alone is good."

That took me back. *Whoa, huh . . . well . . . okay, I can live with that. He's being humble, deflecting the compliment. That's cool. I guess I shouldn't be too surprised. I can see humility is a big deal for him . . . And yeah, of course only God is good . . . Well, I mean . . . I'm not too bad. I mean, I'm pretty good, myself . . . but God is certainly better . . .*

And then he started to walk away. I had to jump up and chase after him. And he turns to me and says, "But concerning your question. You know the commandments, don't you? Don't commit adultery. Don't murder. Don't steal or give false testimony or defraud others. And honor your father and your mother, and love your neighbor."

Ah, good, a checklist.

And as he's rattling off the rules, I'm standing there, thinking, *Check . . . check . . . check . . . okay, so far so good . . .*

I thought back through my life, I really did, and I couldn't remember a single time I'd broken any of those commands. I'm not bragging here; it's just that, like I said, I'm a pretty good person. I've never slept with anyone, murdered anyone, lied, or defrauded others. I've honored my parents. I've shown love to my neighbors. I've been a good, upstanding citizen.

Check . . . check . . . check . . .

"Sir," I said. "I've kept those rules all my life, ever since I can remember. Ever since I was a little kid."

I figured he'd slap me on the back and congratulate me and say something like, "Nice! If you've kept the rules that well, you'll get to heaven for sure. Everyone knows that people who are pretty good make it to heaven, and only really bad people go down below. Good job!"

But he didn't say that. Not at all.

Instead he looked at me for a long moment and then nodded.

"Then there's one last thing you need to do," he said. And the strange thing was, as he looked at me, I could see something in his eyes that I'd never seen in the eyes of any other religious leader. It went beyond admiration or concern or respect. It wasn't like he was judging me or looking down on me or anything. It was almost like the look my dad used to give me when he was alive, back when I was a boy . . .

Love? Was it love in his eyes?

"Go and sell what you have," he said. "Sell it all and give the money to the poor. If you do that, you'll have treasure in heaven. Then come and follow me."

His words stunned me.

Sell everything? But I've earned this stuff! I've worked hard for it! I just stood there blinking, looking at him, trying to figure out if he was just exaggerating to make a point or if he really meant it.

I opened my mouth to say something, but nothing came out. I glanced at the people there, and they were studying me carefully.

At first I was angry. *Who are you to tell me how to get to heaven, anyway? How dare you?!* But then I remembered I was the one who'd come to him with the question in the first place.

Then I was confused. *How could I get to heaven by doing that? What does giving away all I own have to do with heaven? And then I have to come and follow you? Are you telling me I can't get to heaven without following you?!*

In the end I was just plain sad as I realized his plan didn't really fit in with my career goals. How could I give up everything I'd spent my life working for, everything I'd lived for, just because he said to?

I couldn't.

I wouldn't.

So I nodded my thanks to him and walked away. He didn't have what I was looking for. Or maybe I should say, he didn't tell me what I wanted to hear.

Sell *some* things—that I could handle. Give *more* to the poor—no problem. But everything?

That's not reasonable. That's asking too much.

I guess for everyone there's a limit when it comes to being religious. A breaking point, you know? There's only so far a person can go. And then you just gotta trust in how good you've been to make up for the rest. I guess that's where I was at.

But still . . . his words wouldn't leave me alone.

"Only God is good . . ."

What's that about? What's he trying to tell me? That being good is never good enough? Could that be true? I mean, of course only God is Good—Good with a capital G—everyone knows that . . . but doesn't pretty good count for something? Or have all of my efforts over all this time been wasted? I've been trying to follow the rules my whole life. Has it all been wasted? Has my whole life been spent in the pursuit of . . . nothing?!

His words still haunt me—that and the look in his eyes. It was love. I know that now. A love so deep that it realized I didn't want to follow him. I wanted to go my own way instead. A love so deep that it let me.

Sometimes I wonder what it would have been like if I had actually done what he suggested—if I'd sold everything and followed him. I wonder where I'd be today. I wonder what my future would hold, how things would be different.

Actually, ever since I died and came here, that's all I can think of. Those words of his, filling my head, echoing throughout the corridors of this place forever . . .

Only God is good . . .

Only God . . .

Only God . . .

Then come and follow me . . .

Nope. I was wrong about money. There's one thing it cannot buy.

Money cannot buy eternity.

I used to think, *I can always sell my stuff and follow Jesus tomorrow. Later on, you know, after I've made my mark on the world. After all, I'm a young guy, and I've got my whole life ahead of me.*

But the truth is, I didn't have my whole life ahead of me. No one does. We have our whole lives behind us. What we have ahead of us is a mystery that could be over at any moment.

It didn't take people long to finish paying their last respects and then file away, to go back to their jobs and their busy, busy lives. And it won't be long before they forget all about me. After all, I wasn't that important—not in the big scheme of things. In a few years no one will even remember my name.

But I'll remember his. As hard as I try, I'll never be able to forget about him.

Oh, dear God . . .

. . . what have I done? . . .

making it personal

Jesus looked at him and loved him. "One thing you lack," he said. "Go, sell everything you have and give to the poor, and you will have treasure in heaven. Then come, follow me." At this the man's face fell. He went away sad, because he had great wealth.

—Mark 10:21-22

This man had great wealth—and greater poverty. He was rich in many ways but poor in the most important way. As Jesus said once, "What good will it be for a man if he gains the whole world, yet forfeits his soul?" (Matthew 16:26).

What good indeed?

Two things were keeping this man from receiving eternal life. First, he was trapped by the illusion that he himself was good enough to get into heaven. But only God is good. That's the kicker. Not us. Just God, only God. Until we realize that, we'll never be spiritually rich. We'll never be able to follow Jesus. Within those few words is a truth so sharp it cuts all of our excuses away—if only we're brave enough to admit it.

Secondly, the man's love for the things of this world overshadowed his love for the things of God. Jesus promised him heavenly treasure if he would only open up his heart wide enough to receive it. But he wouldn't. If you love this life and the things of this life more than the life of following Jesus, you'll never get to heaven. Period.

This man had wrapped his life so tightly around the things of this world that he wasn't ready to let go. But the spiritual life is a process of untangling ourselves from our attachments to this world, not entwining ourselves even further within them. Our hearts are not big enough to hold both God and the world. It's either one or the other.

As long as we love stuff more than we love Jesus, we'll never have eternal life. Jesus invites us to die to the world, not to clutter our hearts with its jagged trinkets.

You can't add Jesus to your life and have everything else remain the same. It won't happen that way. He asks for all of your devotion, affection, commitment, service, love, and worship. All of it. You can't divide those things up between him and the world. It's either one or the other. There is no compromise, no wiggle room. Your life will either be spent in the service of materialism or of God.

That young man chose what would come first in his life. Jesus offers the same choice to each of us—either the world or the Son. Which do you choose?

taking it deeper

1. How do you measure success: money? grades? winning? power? popularity? According to how society measures success, was Jesus successful? Why do you say that? How do you think Jesus measures success?

2. People often talk about pursuing or attaining "the good life." What is the good life? How would you define it? How would Jesus?

3. According to Matthew 6:24, can you serve both God and money? What implications does that have for your life?

4. Why do you think Jesus let this man walk away? Was this guy ready to follow Jesus? When is someone finally ready to follow Jesus?

5. Read Luke 9:23-25. List the requirements Jesus mentions for

following him. Have you done them? If not, can you really call yourself a follower of Jesus?

6.   The man in this story needed to do three things: (1) honestly admit his shortcomings and sins; (2) get over his love affair with the things of this world; and (3) follow Jesus wherever he might lead. Do you agree or disagree that those who follow Jesus today must do the same? How do you feel about that? What will you do about it?

7.   Would you be willing to give everything away if it meant going to heaven? If not, how much would you be willing to give up? How much is heaven worth to you? If you're not willing yet, would you be willing to be made willing?

8.   Jesus wasn't saying that poor people go to heaven—it's just that they usually have less to get in the way of their coming to God. So what is the key to eternal life? (See John 5:24 and 17:3.)

9.   Does Jesus ever allow people to give him some of their lives, a part of their hearts, a fraction of their love, or a sliver of their time? What Bible verses back up your claim? What does that mean for your life today?

breaking free

Good Teacher,
i've got a lot to learn about what it means to be good.
help me to see that only God is good. only you are good.
        and i am not.
i want to be good
i try to be good
        but i am not.
and it isn't simply
that i haven't been good.
it's that
        i
                am
                        not
                                good.

i need your goodness. cover me. forgive me. help me.
and when i've loved stuff instead of you,
        when i need to sell it or give it away or throw it away,
help me to do just that.
drive the world out of my heart,
and make room for you instead.

give me the courage to surrender myself
and hand my life over to you.
amen.

the last to leave
CHAPTER NINE

(John 8:1-11)

Even though it was early in the day, the sun was already higher than it should have been. Blazing hot. Too hot. It made you uncomfortable just to be outside.

I remember 'cause I could feel the sweat forming on my forehead as I watched. As I listened. As I clenched my rock.

A crowd had already gathered. Everyone was picking up rocks, tossing them gently into the air, feeling their weight, judging the distance. The teachers had pushed a woman toward the Nazarene. She was lying on the ground, clinging to a blanket, but other than that, it didn't look like she was wearing anything at all.

I shook my head. Must've caught her in the act. They must have been waiting for her. And now they were bringing her to Jesus.

A breeze. That's what we needed. A breeze to blow away the heat and cool things down. I wiped the sweat off my forehead.

But no breeze came that day. I can still hear the shouting and the curses. I can still feel the fury rise in my chest. I can still remember what it felt like to stand there, ready to throw my stone at her face.

Sweaty and hot.

Waiting for the prophet to reply.

Sh'ma Yisra'el, Adonai Elohaynu, Adonai E'hod.

("Hear, O Israel: The Lord our God, the Lord is one." Deuteronomy 6:4)

From the time I was a young boy, I prayed those words four times every day—two times each morning, then in the evening, and again at bedtime. I hoped that one day I would be praying them when I breathed my last breath. Those are the words that were spoken over me at the moment of my birth. They live and breathe the very essence of the Law of the Lord.

Hear, O Israel: The Lord our God, the Lord is one.

I've always taken God seriously. His Law. His rules. His regulations. Because I love being a Jew. I love the idea of being one of God's chosen people. I love the thought that we're set apart. Different.

A nation chosen by God.

"Jacob!" It was my mother. "The mutton! The mutton! What— have you already forgotten what I sent you outside for?"

I sighed.

"Obey your mother," called my dad. "You know she's not feeling well. Then you can join me in the fields afterward."

"Yes, sir."

Sometimes she really gets on my nerves. I guess that's the way it is with all guys my age . . . Anyway, since she'd gotten sick, I was the one who had to help her out.

As I navigated through the dusty streets on my way to the center of the city, I spied some of my friends hurrying to work. I called to them, and they waved back.

Well, I'll be joining them soon enough.

Then I turned the corner, and the market stretched before me.

The smells drew me in. Roasting meat. Spices from distant lands, myrrh and aloe swirling in the breeze. And perfume.

But that wasn't for sale. My eyes landed on a woman standing beside her cart. It was her perfume I smelled.

She smiled. "So, Jacob," she said, "your mother send you to the market again?"

It was kind of embarrassing running errands for your mom. You understand. I nodded and handed the coins to her. I didn't say anything.

"Is she feeling any better?" she asked.

"A little." I didn't really want to talk to her. Even before Mom got sick, I'd heard of this lady. I knew all about her. All the boys did. We'd heard stories about the kind of woman she was, but no one had ever caught her.

"Here you go, Jacob. Say hi to your mom for me."

"I will."

"I'll be praying for her."

I turned away. *A lot of good that'll do,* I thought.

And then I headed back home, still smelling her perfume. Its elegance had a way of catching hold of you. It was stirring and—okay, I'll say it—seductive. She wasn't much older than me, and she knew how to talk to guys. How to move, smile, tease. That much was for sure. She had this soft prettiness that disarmed you and velvety laughter and a lily-soft smile . . .

I caught myself thinking about her. I couldn't help it.

So anyway, that was the day before. Then I worked with my dad all day in the fields. And at night I said my prayers and went to bed, just like always.

Sh'ma Yisra'el, Adonai Elohaynu, Adonai E'hod.

And I dreamed about her that night—the delicate touch of her fingers grazing the back of my hand as she handed me my change, the smell of her perfume. *She could teach you things, Jacob . . . show you things . . .*

I was sweating when I woke up. And that's when I heard the commotion, the shouts. I headed outside.

It was just after dawn, but the Nazarene was already teaching at the courts of the temple. The usual people were there with him, hanging on his every word.

And then, even before the teachers arrived, I heard the news, whispered along the streets. Gossip spreads faster around here than a disease. So by the time I got there, it was tough to even see the Nazarene because of the crowd—everyone holding their rocks, getting ready. The little kids had to hold theirs with both hands.

There was going to be a stoning today before breakfast was even served.

I reached down and found a nice-sized rock. I'd been at stonings before. We all had. It was our way to uphold the law of our land. God's Law.

I cradled the rock in my palm and peered toward the street. The rock felt good in my hand. Nice weight to it. I imagined the kind of damage a rock like this could do with a good, direct hit. I know it sounds kinda barbaric, but in our land the guilty get what they deserve. It's the Law—God's Law. Justice is as swift as a rock launched toward your head.

But who was it? Who had they caught? Who would we stone on this steamy, hot morning?

I eased forward.

My friends Ari and Josiah stood nearby, choosing rocks of their own. They looked toward me, and I held out my hand to show off the rock I'd found. They nodded and held up theirs. We all smiled.

The Nazarene had stopped teaching. He turned and faced the crowd.

That's when I saw the teachers—my teachers—arriving. They were stone-faced. Grim. Solemn. Serious about their job as God's spokesmen. Deadly serious. Just like they should be. But I saw something else on their faces. A smirk? A hint of arrogance? It was tough to be sure. And then they shoved a woman toward the Nazarene.

I could smell her perfume floating toward me through the hot air. A swirl of emotions swept through me, and I knew.

It's the woman from the market! The one you dreamed about last night!

So the stories were true after all. She trembled in the dust, clutching her blanket.

I shook my head and locked my fingers around the stone.

And now they'd brought her to the Nazarene.

I wiped a drop of sweat from my brow. Somewhere a dog barked.

The Nazarene turned and faced them. I watched. He looked at the leaders and then at the woman lying there, shaking in the dust.

Her lips were quivering. Her hands shook. She knew what was coming. She knew what the stones were for. She stared at the dirt.

And then one of the teachers, one of my teachers, smiled. His name was Shimon Ben Zakkai.

"Rabbi," he said. You could hear the disdain in his voice as he spit out the word. "This woman was caught *in the act of adultery.*"

He spoke slowly and deliberately, savoring every word, tasting them on his tongue. "The Law of Moses says that we must kill her." He paused for effect and looked around. He was playing to the crowd. Finally, he let his eyes land on the Nazarene. Rabbi Zakkai was controlling the moment. He knew it and he liked it. "What do you say we should do with her?"

His words hung in the air like icicles. No one moved. I shivered for a moment, even in the blazing heat.

the last to leave

Yes, what do you say we should do with her? I thought. *The Law is clear—death by stoning. You're the one who goes around claiming to be sent from God. You're the one who gives us all these new teachings and interpretations of the Law. What do you say, Rabbi? What should we do?*

As Rabbi Zakkai's words slowly sank to the ground, all the whisperings in the crowd faded away. We stopped tossing our rocks up and down. It was almost like the morning was holding its breath. Somewhere behind me someone coughed.

I stared at the Nazarene. He talked a lot about judgment. I'd never heard anyone talk so much about hell until this guy came along. But he also talked a lot about forgiveness—the forgiveness of God and the forgiveness we're supposed to share with others. It all sounded nice in theory, I'll admit it.

But I couldn't see it ever working in the real world.

My teachers had told me all about him. They explained how he subverted the people. They said his teachings were dangerous. That he was the bastard son of a peasant girl and had no right to tell anyone, especially them, what to believe about God. Still, when he challenged them to find anything in his life that didn't measure up to his teachings, they couldn't do it. I remembered that, too.

So now they had the chance to discredit him for good, here in front of everyone. This man who spoke about loving others as much as you love yourself. Let's see him get out of this one. Would he condemn her? If he did, he'd lose credibility. All his talk about forgiveness would be proven to be just that—talk. But if he didn't condemn her, he'd be speaking heresy. Going against the very Law of God.

Sure, the teachers were setting him up. I could see that. We all could. But it was about time. He had to be stopped. And this woman was the perfect way to end it all.

It would end for both of them here. Today.

Her perfume drifted toward me, both sweet and sour at the same time, both alluring and repulsive. She was crying.

The Nazarene looked at her, shaking there in the dirt, clinging to her blanket. Then he looked at the Pharisees and other religious teachers standing in front of him.

He actually took the time to look into the eyes of each of them. One at a time.

We waited, standing in the blazing heat. He wasn't in any hurry.

I shifted my weight to the other foot.

The sun raged above us. Still, the Nazarene was quiet.

What's going on? Is he stalling? Evaluating his options? Why doesn't he say something?!

But what could he say, after all? If he told us to stone her, all of his followers would think he was too harsh, too judgmental, too much like all the other teachers. They'd leave him because he was no different.

But if he told us not to . . . well, he'd be going against the Law handed down to us from God himself. That was blasphemy. There would be two stonings here today.

Then without saying a word, he bent down and wrote something in the dirt with his finger.

Some people leaned forward to see what he was writing.

What kind of an answer is that? Drawing in the sand?!

From where I was standing, I couldn't read what he was writing. Later, some people said he was jotting down the commandments, one at a time. Others said he was writing the names of all the teachers, listing 'em one by one. No one seemed to know for sure.

The air was impossibly hot. I eased my finger under the collar of my tunic and tugged.

Even the woman who'd been whimpering softly and crying into the blanket was quiet now. She peered at the prophet bent over, writ-

the last to leave

ing beside her. Her face was smeared with dirty tears. She shook softly on the ground.

"What do you say?" barked Rabbi Zakkai. "Don't ignore us! Give us an answer! The people are waiting! We're all waiting!" He gestured toward us like a politician giving a speech.

Then the Nazarene nodded. He looked up at last and said, "All right then. Go ahead. Stone her—"

So he's just like the others, after all!

I began cocking back my arm, sliding my body through the crowd. Into position. My rock would be the first to land.

But the Nazarene wasn't done. He said the next words with a quiet confidence that still haunts me: "Anyone here who's without sin, go ahead and throw the first stone."

What?!

And then the Nazarene just went back to scribbling in the sand.

I froze. No one knew what to do. No one moved. No one spoke. Not even my friend Ari, and he always has something to say.

I searched the eyes of Shimon Ben Zakkai. He was the one who'd taught me God's Law. He was the one who'd taught me how to pray.

How's he gonna respond to the words of the Nazarene?

My teacher opened his mouth quickly, as if he were going to argue with the Nazarene, but then he just stood there, his mouth gaping open. He closed it and then opened it again and then closed it one last time very slowly. A few moments ago his eyes had been smug and self-assured. But not anymore. Something passed in front of his face. I could see a tempest brew beneath his skin, as if he were rereading ages and ages of the Law in an instant, as if he were rethinking life itself. His face quivered slightly and then . . .

. . . then . . .

. . . he dropped his rock. It slipped from his grip and landed with a soft thud on the sandy ground beside his feet.

What? What are you doing?!

Slowly, he lowered his head and backed up. A shuffle at first, then a quicker step. He was leaving. He was walking away! He disappeared behind me into the crowd, pulling a swirl of the woman's perfume in his wake.

The Nazarene didn't look up.

What's going on?

Rabbi Zakkai had been the one to teach me that our God is a God of justice! And that justice means making sure people get what they deserve! Why was he leaving now? There was justice to be served!

Then the words from an ancient psalm of David echoed in my head, a psalm I had learned at synagogue last year: "The Lord is compassionate and gracious, slow to anger, abounding in love. He will not always accuse, nor will he harbor his anger forever; he does not treat us as our sins deserve or repay us according to our iniquities."

Compassion. Grace. Love. Forgiveness. Mercy.

But can justice and mercy really dwell together in the same heart? Can they really live together in the same God? Can judgment and forgiveness really be spoken in the same breath?

For a few moments no one else moved. But then, the other teachers began to drop their rocks or set them down and ease away into the background. They all lowered their eyes as they left. None of them had the guts to look at the Nazarene.

Still, he hadn't looked up from the ground.

That's when I realized he hadn't been slow to answer in order to stall. He'd done it to let them simmer, to let them think. And now he was drawing in the sand to let 'em leave without having to look him in the eye . . . He knew . . . he'd known all along what he was going to say! Before he ever leaned over to draw in the dirt . . . he already knew! He had done it just for impact.

Who is this man?

Can judgment and forgiveness really be spoken in the same breath?

Rage boiled inside of me.

No!

The word cut through my mind. I think I even said it aloud because a few people looked at me as the crowd thinned out.

Who does he think he is? How dare he! So self-righteous! I felt like throwing my rock at him!

No one is without sin, Nazarene! Where do you get off talking like that? If you're so perfect why don't you toss a rock at her? I'll tell you why—because you're afraid. Gutless!

Why was he skirting around the clear dictates of God's Law? Only a heretic looks for loopholes!

Justice never requires the judge to be sinless, Nazarene! Justice makes sure people get what they deserve!

But then once again I remembered those words of David. They stabbed at me like living daggers: "The Lord . . . will not always accuse . . . He does not treat us as our sins deserve or repay us according to our iniquities." *Mercy gives us all a second chance . . .*

One by one they left. One by one they walked away. The oldest men left first, the grandfathers and elders and teachers. Then the fathers and husbands, the bearded ones. Then their sons. Until it was only my friends and me. I looked at them and tried to say with my eyes, "Don't let him get away with this! Don't let him do it!"

But then Josiah—and even Ari—set down their rocks. They walked away, leaving me alone with Jesus and the woman.

The rock felt heavy in my hand.

I could still do it. I could still stone her. It was my right. The Law couldn't touch me. The Law was on my side! Yes! Yes, I would be the one! I would be the one to stand up for the Law! Yes!

I would be the one to hurl my rock at her forehead! I wouldn't let the Nazarene get away with this!

The Lord our God, the Lord is one!

But what would people think of you—that you think you're sinless? Is that it? Do you really think you're without sin? Are you really ready to throw that stone?

Jesus hadn't moved. He still stared at the dust. I looked around at the eyes peering at us through windows. I felt dizzy.

His words echoed in my head.

"Anyone here who's without sin, go ahead and throw the first stone."

My arm began to quiver. *You can't throw it, Jacob. You're not without sin. You're just like her . . . Just like her . . . She was in bed with someone else last night, but you slept with her . . . In your dreams you slept with her . . .*

My rock slipped from my hand, and I stumbled backward. Tears were welling up in my eyes.

Just like her . . . You're just like her . . . All of us are just like her . . . No one is without sin . . . except him . . .

I ran for home, taking one last look back. He was helping her to her feet. He was offering her his outer tunic to cover her nakedness.

What kind of a man is this?

I can still feel the sweat under my collar, still smell the fragrance of her perfume lingering on the edge of the morning—still to this day—swirling around the words of the Nazarene.

And I wonder if I will ever be as transparent as she was. To stand before him, take his hand, and let him cover me.

making it personal

Jesus straightened up and asked her,
"Woman, where are they? Has no one condemned you?"

> "No one, sir," she said.
> "Then neither do I condemn you," Jesus declared.
> "Go now and leave your life of sin."
>
> —John 8:10-11

God isn't out to get you. He's not sitting up in heaven with a big pencil, writing down everything you do wrong, trying to build a case against you. No, he has an eraser instead. He's out to forgive you. He's on your side.

The question is: Are you on his?

The Pharisees thought they'd caught that woman in the act, but Jesus turned the tables and showed them they'd really only caught themselves. None of us is without sin. And that's why all of us need a Savior.

Jesus didn't downplay her sin. He didn't make light of it or tell her it was no big deal. Because it was a big deal. He told her to "leave her life of sin," but he didn't condemn her. He forgave her. As Jesus once said, "For God did not send his Son into the world to condemn the world, but to save the world through him" (John 3:17).

Jesus didn't come to lay a guilt trip on us or make us feel worthless and no good. He came to forgive. But before our sins can be forgiven, they've gotta be acknowledged. And that's the tough part because it requires courage and gut-wrenching honesty.

Jesus is the great revealer. He doesn't let anyone hide. His justice uncovers, his mercy forgives. His law slays us. His grace saves us.

How?

It's a mystery.

Actually, it's the mystery, *the* biggest mystery of all. The mystery of how God became human, suffered, died, and rose to save us when we trust in him.

Without question, this is the great mystery of our faith: Christ appeared in the flesh and was shown to be righteous by the Spirit.

He was seen by angels and was announced to the nations.
He was believed on in the world and was taken up into heaven.

—1 Timothy 3:16 (NLT)

How can God love the sinner and hate the sin? How can he be merciful and yet remain just? Only through the mystery of Jesus.

We're not asked to comprehend it. We're not asked to understand it. We're only asked to accept him, believe him, and let him cover our nakedness, too.

taking it deeper

1. Who do you identify with most in this story—the woman, the rabbi, Jesus, or the guy holding the rock? Why?

2. Read this story for yourself in John 8:1-11. What details strike you? What surprises you?

3. Imagine being there that day—being the last one to leave. What would have been going through your head? Would you have dropped your rock, or thrown it at the woman? Why?

4. The teens were the last ones to drop their rocks and walk away. What does that tell you about them? What does it tell you about yourself?

5. If you were there that day, what might you and your friends have talked about later in the day? How would the events of that morning have shaped your view of Jesus? Your view of yourself?

6. Jesus could have thrown a rock that day. After all, he was without sin. Why didn't he? Think about it. Do you think his restraint showed weakness or strength? Can you think of any other times he restrained his power because of his love? (Hint: See Matthew 26:52-54.) What does that show you about his character?

7. Read Romans 3:19-20. What is the main purpose of God's law—to reveal our sin to us or to give us a set of guidelines so that we can work our way to heaven? How do these verses relate to this story?

the last to leave

8. That day the woman got a second chance. In what area of your life do you need a second chance? Will you accept the one God is offering to you right now?

breaking free

Nazarene,
the rock feels heavy in my hand.
i want to throw it at others.
help me look more deeply at myself!

let the rock slip away.
 let the admissions and honesty come.
  for i am more like that woman than i care to admit.
right now, in this moment,
i need to hear you say those words,
"neither do i condemn you . . . "

i must drop my rock
for i know that if i throw it,
it will only end up hitting me.

cool the heat of the law's conviction,
help me feel the forgiving breeze of your Spirit.
lift me to my feet and cover me;
and help me to leave my life of sin, too.
amen.

fury

CHAPTER TEN

(Mark 11:15-19)

It was late afternoon, almost quittin' time. I didn't really expect to do any more business that day. So I was just relaxing on my bench, watching the other vendors herd together their sheep and cattle, pack up their crates and their coins, and head out of the temple area. Another day, another dollar.

Just then a really intense-looking rabbi wearing a hand-me-down tunic that was way too small for him walked into the courtyard. He was leading a group of men who looked like they'd just gotten off work at the dockyards.

None of 'em looked like they had very much money.

Oh, well, I thought. *Who knows? Maybe I can make a couple bucks off these yahoos before calling it a day. At least they look like they've got plenty of sins to atone for!*

"Shalom!" I called, standing up and waving. "Shalom! Welcome to the city of David! Glorious day today! Glorious day!" The man and his crew stopped and looked my way. His dark eyes scanned my piles of coins, my ledger, my caged doves.

I smiled wide, showing him my mouth full of teeth.

Most guys in their late teens start losing their teeth. Not me. Nope. I take good care of my chompers. When you're working in sales, there's nothing as persuasive as a big, bright smile.

"Can I sell you a dove today? No better time than now for a little sacrifice! Or maybe buy one now for later in week! Beat the Passover rush!" I gestured toward my inventory of sacrificial doves. "No better doves anywhere! No better doves at all!" Then I leaned real close and whispered, "I'll cut you and your buddies a deal, give you the best exchange rates in the courtyard . . ." I winked at him. I had him. I knew it. I figured them for at least half a dozen doves. I smiled again.

But he did not smile back. He just took a deep breath and glared at me. The muscles in his face started twitching and quivering. And then, through tightly pressed lips, he said one word.

"No."

Only then did I notice his rough, muscular hands curling into fists and the veins popping out of those massive forearms that his tunic refused to cover. I took a step backward.

Maybe this guy's not a rabbi after all! Maybe he's a freedom fighter. Or an escaped convict. Maybe he's a bandit with a pack of thieves!

His hands opened and closed, opened and closed, muscles flexing. Almost as if a wild beast were crawling beneath his skin.

Okay, that's weird. The guy was starting to scare me . . .

He mouthed the word again.

"No."

I eased back. "Right, of course. Well, too late for a sacrifice today anyway. No probl—"

The man in the next booth over cut me off.

"Hey! Aren't you that rabbi?" he says. "That Jesus guy everyone's talking about?! You are, aren't you? I know you are! Say, can you sign my scroll for me? My kid can't stop talking about you. He's one of your biggest fans! It'd mean a lot to him! Really!" He held a parchment and a pen toward the man.

People in the crowd began to look our way.

Then the man spun on his heels, kicking up a cloud of dust. He looked around one more time at the temple courtyard, the sheep, the cattle, the businessmen. Then he said the word again, louder this time—loud enough to still the conversations in every direction.

"NO!"

The word echoed behind him as he stomped off with his men. They never even opened their mouths.

"Well, you don't have to be rude about it!" yelled the guy, holding his limp piece of paper. "Jeez."

I looked around. Even the animals had stopped moving to watch him leave. No one was laughing. Whatever this man was, he was no joke.

Huh . . . I thought as I packed up my things. *What was that all about?*

I didn't have to wait long to find out. Because the very next morning, right after we'd all set up shop and were starting to sell our animals—just tryin' to make a living, mind you—striking deals and exchanging people's money, he showed up again.

And this time his friends cowered back.

He burst into the courtyard alone and with a shout. He reminded me of a crazed shepherd trying to drive a pack of wild animals from his flock.

"Out!" he bellowed. "Get out!" And I heard the sharp crack of a whip.

What on earth is goin' on?

"Robbers! Thieves! Out of my Father's house!" he hollered, grabbing a table covered with coins and papers and flipping it over. The papers took flight and shot crazily in all directions. Coins rolled and scampered across the ground. A few fellas started chasing after 'em.

Crack! It was the whip again. He was carrying a whip!

fury

What's he doing? This guy's crazy! I'm gettin' outta here!

I reached for my bags of money just as he got to my table. He looked at me with those cold, angry eyes: "How dare you?" he demanded.

His words cut into me. I wondered if he might be possessed by a demon.

I let go of my money. "What?" I gasped. "What have I done?"

"This is a house of prayer," he breathed between clenched teeth. "And you!" he pointed the whip at me. "You have turned it into a den of robbers!"

I swallowed hard. He raised the whip, and I didn't wait around to find out how good his aim was. I turned and bolted, leaving everything behind. My cages . . . my doves . . . my balance sheets . . . the contents of my bladder . . .

And, yeah, even my money.

Behind me I could hear a crash as my table went flying across the courtyard. Chickens and sheep were skittering everywhere; doves were flapping past my face (probably *my* doves). People were running in circles, hollering. Some folks were even shouting and clapping! People were actually cheering!

It was a madhouse.

He's crazy! I thought. *A raving lunatic!*

Some vendors were trying to carry their goods and money out of the courtyard to escape, but he was stopping 'em at the door. Knocking the merchandise from their hands, kicking their stuff away from 'em. Nobody was fighting back. No one dared to.

And all the while he was carrying on about how we were defiling God's house by turning a house of prayer into a den of robbers.

But I haven't turned anything into a den of robbers! I'm just tryin' to make a living here! You know, pay the bills! I mean, sure, we jack up the prices a little bit at certain times of year. Why not? A person has to make a profit! We're just tryin' to help people worship God! That's all!

That's what I told myself as I left, as I ran from the man with the whip.

Somebody oughta lock that guy up. He's dangerous. A real fanatic!

I thought about all my lost profits. How was I gonna replace my inventory in time for the Passover? This was my busiest week of the year!

Don't worry, I told myself. *Things'll settle down again. Once they catch this joker and lock him up, we can get back to normal around here. That's the important thing—getting back to normal. Getting back to business as usual.*

Yeah, that's the important thing. Getting back to business as usual.

And so, with those thoughts comforting me, I set off to buy some more doves.

making it personal

And as he taught them, he said, "Is it not written: 'My house will be called a house of prayer for all nations'? But you have made it 'a den of robbers.'"
—Mark 11:17

I love how Mark says, "as he taught them."

That was some lesson, being chased out of the church at the end of a whip by the country's leading spiritual teacher. Chew on that for a while.

I mean, what could possess a man of peace to fashion a whip and clear the building? Jesus had walked into the temple the previous day, looked around, and then left the city before coming back in the morning with the whip (Mark 11:11). And what did he do that night?

Well, I think he spent the time making that whip himself. (See John 2:15.)

You see, this cleansing the temple thing was personal. It wasn't just some knee-jerk reaction. It was planned out. Premeditated.

But why? What possessed him to do it?

His passion for God. Jesus was so completely consumed with loving God that when people made a mockery out of worship, it enraged him. That's how seriously he took prayer. That's how much he loved the Father.

This rage, this wrath of God, is something we don't hear much about at churches anymore. The love of God? Sure. Everyone talks about that. But the wrath of Jesus? It almost sounds like a contradiction in terms.

But it's not a contradiction—it's not even a mystery.

Because a lover defends his beloved. He stands up for her. He protects her reputation even if it's ruinous to his own. You don't insult the beloved in the presence of the lover, or if you do you'll face the consequences. Anger and love are cousins: Only those who care ever get angry.

And the more deeply you love something, the more deeply your passion will resonate. If you love justice, you'll be angered at injustice. If you love unborn children, you'll be enraged by abortion. If you love the environment, you'll be mad about pollution. If you love God, you'll be incensed at sin. Anger always and only runs as deep as love. (Incidentally, the same is true about self-love. If you only get angry at inconveniences, insults, and setbacks against you, it's because you love yourself so much.)

Jesus wove that whip with the fury of his love for God. Jesus had a fierce and unrelenting love for his Father—a love that would not be quieted and could not be stilled.

The question for us is: Which end of the whip do we find ourselves on? His end, consumed with a passion for purity and prayer? Or the other end, consumed only with thoughts of ourselves?

taking it deeper

1. All four Gospel writers record Jesus driving out the money changers. (Many Bible scholars say John is describing a different event since he places the story at the beginning of Jesus' ministry, rather than at the end.) Read the stories for yourself in Matthew 21:12-13, Mark 11:11-19, Luke 19:45-46, and John 2:13-17. What surprises you most about these accounts? Is this the picture of Jesus most churches paint?

2. Why don't people talk about the anger of Jesus much today? What are some of the other times Jesus got angry? (Check out Matthew 23, Mark 3:5-6, and Mark 10:13-16 for some ideas.) In your own words how would you describe the things that made Jesus the most angry? Do these things appear in your life? If they do, what will you do about this?

3. What gets you angry—the same things that anger Jesus or just stuff that inconveniences you? What does that tell you about yourself?

4. What consumes you—zeal for God or zeal for yourself? A passion for prayer or a passion for possessions? What makes you weep and pound the table? What do you love enough to furiously defend?

5. Jesus was consumed with zeal for God. He did nothing half-heartedly. (Remember, only those who care ever get angry.) What about you? How does your commitment measure up? What does God think of half-hearted commitment? (See Revelation 3:15-17.)

fury

6. What does 1 Corinthians 6:19-20 say that believers are? If that's true, then what might Jesus want to drive out of your life? What transactions are going on in your soul that shouldn't be? What does the whip of his love need to attack?

7. Will you help him to begin driving those things out today?

breaking free

O Whip-Wielding Carpenter,
rarely does my passion for God take over my life.
rarely does my concern to see people pray
set me on fire.
most of the time, i just have passion for pleasure,
    and comforts,
    and convenience,
    and self.

i usually think of you as a man of love,
not a man of fury.
    but your anger is evidence of your love for God;
    your wrath is evidence of your passion for purity.
let that passion arise in me, also—
against injustice,
and prejudice,
and sacrilege,
and complacency.
    both in the lives of others
    and especially in this heart of mine.

i am consumed by so many things,
let me be consumed by you.
amen.

just helping things along
CHAPTER ELEVEN

(Matthew 10:8; 26:20-25, 45-56; Luke 10:18-20)

Her scream sent a chill rippling down my spine.

A crowd was beginning to form now. All their eyes were on me.

"In the name of Jesus!" I yelled, placing my hands on her shoulders just as I'd seen my master do. "In the name of Jesus, the Son of Man, be gone, I tell you! Get out of her!"

The demon threw her to the ground so hard I heard the bones in her arm crack.

"No!" I said.

"Look what you've done!" laughed a voice rising from the girl's throat.

"Stop it!" I cried. "Don't hurt her! She's innocent!"

"Innocent!" hissed the demon. "Do not speak to me of innocence!" It raised her from the waist up, letting her hover for an instant. Her eyes rolled back inside her head. Then it threw her down again, harder than before. Her limp body slammed to the ground so hard that two fractured bones burst through the skin of her left forearm.

"Blood!" it screeched. "See? And it's all your fault! You better do something about it!"

Just then my partner, Matthew, came running over. I'd started to cast out this demon without him.

"What are you doing!" he yelled. "Stop talking to it and cast it out!"

By then there was quite a crowd. Yes, now I could finish.

"In the name of Jesus, the Son of Man, be gone!" I yelled, loud enough for everyone in the crowd to hear me. Finally, with a blood-curdling cry, the demon shrieked and left the girl. She lay on the ground, pale and lifeless. Matthew knelt over her, moving his hands across her arm, whispering a prayer, healing her.

"She'll be okay," he said at last. "Praise God for the grace of Jesus."

I stood there panting, half out of breath. I had told a demon what to do. A demon! Just like Jesus did! I had authority over demons. I had power over them!

When we got back and told Jesus the news, he shook his head. "Don't celebrate that you have power over demons," he said, looking at Matthew and the others as he spoke. "Rather rejoice that your names are written in heaven's book."

But how could you not celebrate it? How could anyone not celebrate power like that?!

———————————

"C'mon over here," said Jesus, gesturing. "Sit next to me."

I smiled. Yes. *He wants me to sit next to him. He has chosen me.*

As I took my place at the Passover table, my rightful place by his side, I thought back over the years. Everything was finally coming together.

I'd been waiting for the Messiah my whole life. Waiting and waiting and waiting. And then when I met Jesus, I thought the wait was finally over.

He chose me, along with 11 others.

He called himself the "Son of Man." It was kinda quirky and a little weird, but hey, you gotta define yourself, right? As far as titles go, he could have done a lot worse.

And there was something different about him. You could see it right from the start. He had charisma. Guts. A vision for the future. All the things a natural-born leader needs. All the things the Messiah, the Great Deliverer, would have.

You see, our nation had been under the thumb of the Roman Empire for decades. We all longed to be free, to be delivered. And God had made us a promise centuries ago that he would send a mighty conqueror to lead us to a new way of life. That's who we were waiting for. The promised Messiah.

So did I think Jesus was the Messiah? Well, let me put it this way: I thought he had the potential to be the Messiah. He had the tools. But he needed someone to help guide his career. He was a little unrefined. Blunt. Irreverent. Sometimes, down-right rude. But I would help change all that. I would help him, so that he could help us.

My name is Judas. And he chose me.

I admit I was kinda surprised when he put me in charge of the money. Matthew wasn't too happy about that. I mean, he was an accountant, after all. Before he signed on with Jesus, he used to balance the books for the Empire.

Matt even mentioned it to me one day when we were out on the road together preaching repentance, healing, and casting out demons. I'd left the ledger out, and he was paging through it.

"What are you doing?" I asked.

"Judas!?" he exclaimed, obviously startled. I had surprised him. I liked that. "Um, it looks like some of these figures are off. Let me take a closer look at this."

I smiled. "I can handle it, Matt."

just helping things along

He glared at me. He hated it when I called him Matt.

"The numbers are right." I said, closing up the ledger.

He shook his head. "I should be the one handling the income and expenses, not you."

"I guess Jesus just sees something in me that he doesn't see in you, Matt."

He grumbled something under his breath and walked off. I smiled and put the ledger away.

Yeah, I admit I sometimes used funds for personal matters. But it was always for a good cause. The others just didn't see the big picture. They just couldn't see the forest for the trees. But I could. That's what made me different.

From then on I was more careful about covering my tracks.

I don't remember exactly when things began to change. I guess I first started to wonder about him on the way to Jerusalem. He'd started avoiding the crowds. I could understand it to some extent. I mean, he was getting so well-known that everywhere we went, people would pour out to meet us. It was impressive how little he did for his public image and yet how popular he was.

But I couldn't understand why he didn't rally people to his side. "I didn't come to bring peace," he told us one time. "But a sword."

Yeah, no kidding! I thought. *So start using it!*

He got moody and depressed. His rhetoric changed. He started talking more about suffering and death—not of the Empire but of himself. And he started crying more. At Lazarus' tomb he did it in front of everyone! I started to think maybe he'd lost his nerve.

I mean, it's okay to let people see that you're human—that's good for public relations. But you can't let 'em see you act weak.

Of course, I didn't say anything about it at the time. I'd seen how hard he came down on Peter—calling him "Satan" right to his face—when Pete suggested he shouldn't talk so much about death and dying, but about victory instead.

No, I would be quiet. I would bide my time. I'd keep my peace until everything was just right.

———————

Then earlier this week I thought maybe the time had come.

As we entered the city, the people erupted into praise. They rushed out to greet us. It was just before the Passover celebration, so the city was teeming with people. They were shouting and singing—worshiping the Son of Man!

The Pharisees told Jesus to quiet the crowd, to rein everyone in. But he refused. "If I tell them to be quiet," he said, "the boulders will break into song!"

Yes, Jesus! Yes!

But before it was all over, he was crying again, looking around the city, shaking his head.

What's wrong with you? I thought. *Don't let these people see you like this!*

And then the next day he grabbed a whip and headed to the temple. He drove out the money changers single-handedly. I watched them run from him.

Yes! Overthrow them! Topple the Empire! Free the people! The time has come!

I stood poised by the gate, ready to run to his side.

But once again, in his moment of glory, he dropped the

ball. He just lowered his head, set down the whip, and walked away. He had them on the run! He had the upper hand! The people were rallying to our side! And what does he do? He retreats. I was afraid he might start crying again.

I was stunned. Why didn't he do what we'd come here to do? Overthrow Rome, set up the kingdom, free the people!

Give him a little nudge, I heard a voice whisper in my soul. *Help him along. That's why he chose you. Because you're strong. You're different. Remember that. You're worthy. And so is he. He has never needed you as much as he does now. Be the friend he needs you to be.*

Yes, yes. That's it. I could help. I would give him a nudge.

It's up to you.

It's up to me . . .

———————

He was a powerful man, a man of conviction and authority and passion—that's true—but you can't expect him to be perfect. He was a smart man, but you can't expect him to think of everything.

So anyway, the priests and Pharisees made it easy for me. They told me to name my price, and they had the money ready when I did. They had no idea what their money would buy.

Freedom.

Freedom from Rome. Freedom for us all.

———————

So after I took my seat by his side, we began the Passover meal. He was upset. That much was clear. Finally, after talking about blood and suffering again, he passed the wine around. And then he was overcome with sadness.

Oh, boy. Here come the tears again.

"One of you will betray me," he said softly.

So he knew. Somehow he'd found out.

It's not a betrayal, Jesus. You'll see. I'm just helping things along. You'll thank me for it later.

Questions rounded the table. "Who?" we asked under our breath. "Is it me? Surely, it's not me?"

I reached for a piece of bread, and he put his hand on mine.

And then he whispered to me, "What you are planning to do, do quickly."

I smiled. "I will."

Yes, yes, I will. I know that you need me! I won't let you down!

I got up from the table and left the room.

――――――

We met in secret.

"It's about time," barked one of the priests. "What took you so long?"

"I had to be careful. Make sure I wasn't followed."

He grunted. "Where is he, then?"

"We have to wait for him to leave the house," I said. "It might start a riot if you arrest him there. Trust me. You have to trust me. He'll go outside the city later to pray. You can do it then."

The priest scowled at me. "I still don't understand why you're willing to turn him over to us. Aren't you supposed to be his friend?"

just helping things along

He has no idea! It's because I am his friend that I'm doing this! Because I'm being the best friend a leader ever had!

I hid a grin. "Sometimes people step over the line. Sometimes they go too far. And when they do, you need to put things back in order."

He looked at me, grunted again, and then walked away.

It was all so perfect! They were paying me to help him, not hurt him! We could never overpower Rome in the city. They'd have troops there in a minute! But outside the city— in the gardens, in the darkness! It would be to our advantage! The final revolt would start there and gain momentum, and then we could move into the city, take control, and stand up to the Roman Empire once and for all!

Everything was going according to plan.

After a few hours had passed, I figured he would certainly have left the house. He'd told us earlier to meet him in the place of prayer. We all knew the place. He didn't have to say anything more. We'd been there lots of times. I knew right where he meant.

And so I led the crowd through the night. Ah, they followed me everywhere! I even took the long route just to enjoy the feeling of all those people following me. Me! They would go wherever I told them! It was just a taste of things to come.

There he was. In the moonlight I could tell which one was him. The way he stood. That's how I knew.

"Rabbi," I said. I held him. I greeted him. I kissed him.

He whispered to me, "My friend, do what you came to do . . ." He sounded weak.

Yes, my friend! I will!

I nodded to the soldiers. Then I stood back from him for a moment and looked at him at arm's length. *I've done my part, Jesus. Now you do yours! Didn't you come to deliver our people?! Didn't you come to save us? Now set us free!*

The guards stepped forward to arrest him.

And so it begins! I thought.

Peter lunged forward with his sword drawn.

Yes! Yes!

I heard the pained cry of a man as sword met flesh. I saw Jesus pull free from the guards.

Overthrow Rome! Set up the kingdom! Free the people!

I was giddy with power. Drunk with the moment. It was happening just like I'd planned! The moment of freedom had come!

But then the unthinkable happened.

Jesus didn't fight back.

"No, Peter!" he yelled. "I could call down thousands of angels to help me—"

Yes! Power!

"—but then God's plan would never be fulfilled."

What? I don't understand!

Jesus knelt down. He healed the man.

And that was about it. He didn't start a rebellion. He didn't call us to arms. He just held out his hands for them to arrest him. My hands started to shake as I watched.

No! No!

The others all ran away. Even Peter.

No! Not like this! It's not supposed to end like this!

just helping things along

But it did. They led him away. Everything ended that night in the garden.

I won't bore you with the details of the trials and the false witnesses and the early morning tribunals. But as I watched things unfold, I knew it was over. He wasn't the man I'd thought he was.

———————

"Look what you've done!" laughs a voice rising in my soul.

"Stop it!" I cried to the officials. "Don't hurt him! He's innocent!"

But they mocked me, and so did the voice.

"Innocent! Do not speak to me of innocence!"

I watched the beatings. I saw his blood.

"Blood!"

I tried to return the money, but they laughed at me.

"See? And it's all your fault!"

It's all my fault.

"You better do something about it!"

Yes, I will do something about it.

I slide further out on the branch.

I slip the noose around my neck.

There's only one thing left to do. One thing I can do.

I lean forward.

There's a horrible *snap!* and a flash of scarlet pain.

And then all is darkness.

And that's when the real screams begin.

making it personal

Jesus said to her, "I am the resurrection and the life. He who believes in me will live, even though he dies; and whoever lives and believes in me will never die. Do you believe this?"
—John 11:25-26

Judas didn't believe it. He knew Jesus personally, but he didn't believe in him spiritually. Judas heard the words of Jesus, but he listened instead to the lies of Satan. Step by step he walked further and further into the darkness until it engulfed him. He died in loneliness, regret, and despair and then went to hell to relive his anguish over and over again forever.

Judas has gone down in history as the greatest betrayer of all time. So why did he do it? Why did he turn Jesus over? Honestly, we don't know his specific reasons. It may have been greed or anger or ambition or maybe revenge. The same kind of stuff that motivates people today motivated him back then.

We do know the tragic results of his choices, though. After his betrayal he realized Jesus was innocent. He regretted what he'd done and tried to make it right by returning the money. When that didn't work, his guilt and regrets stalked him. They caught up with him on the edge of the town, and he committed suicide before he could discover the grace and forgiveness of the one whom he'd betrayed.

His story should be a wake-up call for all of us. The death of Jesus was not the end, as Judas thought, but only the beginning. God's plan was to conquer death by dying and to offer us life by living again.

He is the resurrection. He is the life. Do you believe that?

Where you spend eternity hinges on your answer to that simple question.

just helping things along

taking it deeper

1. To find out more about Judas, search for his name in an online Bible or in a Bible concordance. Read the verses that mention him. What's your impression of this man? Is it similar to the way he's portrayed in this story? If not, how would you describe him?

2. According to Mark 6:7-13 Judas cast demons out in the name of Jesus, but according to Jesus, even that's not proof of a renewed heart (Matthew 7:21-24). What does Jesus say is the evidence of a changed life and genuine faith? (See John 14:23-24.) Did Judas exhibit that? Do you?

3. There's a difference between regret and repentance. Feeling bad is not the same as admitting that you are bad. Judas had a change of mind but not a change of heart. Judas certainly felt bad about what he'd done, but was that enough to save him? (See John 17:12 and Acts 1:25.)

4. Some people think that Judas was destined to be damned, that he had no choice in the matter, that he couldn't have been saved even if he wanted to. What do Luke 11:13, John 3:16, and 1 Timothy 2:3-4 have to say about that? What hope do these verses offer you?

5. According to those verses, does God want all people to be saved? So whose fault is it that Judas (or anyone else) is condemned?

6. According to 1 John 2:2, did Jesus die for Judas? Did Jesus die for you? How should that affect your life? How does it?

breaking free

Friend, i have kissed your cheek in betrayal,
i have run from your side in denial,
i have watched you suffer in despair.
  and when i look at my regrets,
  they do not fade,

but grow angrier and louder,
as sleek as eels sliding through my soul.

O Jesus, Son of Man,
    lead me back to the light!
    lead me back to the truth!
as shattering as it might be
to the illusions i've pursued,
show me that darkness lies inside of me
and the only sword that works against it
is the one you wield.
slice me open
and let your light transform my soul.
amen.

hour of darkness
CHAPTER TWELVE

(Luke 22:47-53; John 18:10-11)

We all knew the signal. Judas would greet the prophet. We'd seize him, arrest him, and overpower his bodyguards. I gulped as we crossed the Kidron Valley. A chill ran down my spine; I told myself it was from the cold night air.

I clutched my club with both hands as we arrived at the Garden of Gethsemane.

What am I doing here? I'm only a slave to the Jewish high priest! I've never been trained to arrest anyone!

And the last person I wanted to try to arrest was the prophet.

———————————

Back when he first appeared, my master, Caiaphas, and the other religious rulers just mocked him. But then crowds of people began to follow him, and I think Caiaphas and the others felt threatened. Maybe even scared. You see, the people claimed the prophet could do miracles. Like feeding a huge crowd, healing sick people, and even raising dead people to life!

They wanted to get rid of him. So they tried arresting him, intimidating him, making him say something stupid . . . They even tried to stone him to death! But he always got away, and they always ended up looking like fools. Finally, they decided they'd had enough.

That's when they called us.

It was just before the Passover Feast, Thursday night. We were already asleep, but they shook us from our beds and made us gather in the courtyard. We were shocked! Whoever heard of slaves helping arrest a prophet in the middle of the night? Especially during Passover! But the rulers said they thought he might start a revolt, so they wanted numbers.

The Roman soldiers were already there. They looked as scared as we were. Scared of what the Galilean would do. Or could do. If he could raise the dead, what other powers did he hold? It was rumored that his bodyguards were expert swordsmen. And the prophet? Well, some said he was a sorcerer, others a mysterious miracle worker, others a dangerous rebel. I'd even heard rumors that he was a madman who called on the name of demons to do his signs. I didn't know what to think. But I knew I was afraid.

What a crowd! Some carried lanterns, others torches, still others swords or clubs. A man named Judas was our guide. We followed him through the trees to the grove where the Galilean was thought to be hiding.

We stepped into a clearing, and I saw him.

He was talking with three other men. His other followers were probably hiding in ambush. I tightened my grip on the club and glanced at the shadows.

Then the four of them turned toward us. Fear crackled through the night like sparks from a fire. Those with weapons clenched them tightly. Judas approached one of the men and kissed his cheek to greet him. "That's the one," I thought. "That's Jesus." I wasn't sure if I wanted to run from him or bow down before his feet. I knew I did not want to fight him.

In my curiosity, I stepped forward to look at his face.

Before I knew what had happened, the prophet turned to us and asked who we came for. His voice was gentle, yet it echoed with the thunder of the mountains. His question split the night. And then I was looking up from the ground. Had I been pushed? Had I fainted? No, it was the power of his voice! I wasn't alone on the ground. We were all lying there, even the soldiers. We rose, and he repeated the question. Again we fell. Was he mocking us? Who was this man? *What* was this man? A few in the crowd ran off, little lights bouncing through the night.

The men standing by the prophet nervously asked if they should strike with their swords, although they looked as frightened as we were. We just stood there, staring at each other with the prophet between us. Finally, a few guards stepped forward and seized Jesus.

Suddenly, one of his men lunged at me. I ducked to the side as I saw the sword slash toward my head. There were shouts, and swords were drawn. I heard the slicing of metal, but it was muffled. A roaring filled my head. I arose ready to meet the attackers. It was then that I felt the warm flow of blood down my neck. If I hadn't ducked, more than my ear would have fallen to the ground.

A voice silenced the crowd. "Enough! No more of this! Let them do what they came to do."

And then the man from Galilee pulled free from the guards. But he didn't run or strike out at us. He bent down and picked something up from the ground. He held it up against the side of my head, and the roar inside of me ceased. The flow of blood stopped. He healed me. He healed me, even though I had come to lead him to his death.

It was a warm and soothing feeling when he touched me. His finger trailed across my cheek, and then he smiled at me. And he looked into my eyes with a tenderness I've never seen before or since. No wonder the crowds followed him. How could anyone look into his eyes and feel his touch and do otherwise?

That was the last time his hands were ever free.

The guards yanked his arms behind him and tied him up. He said something about his Father and angels and a cup, but I wasn't really listening. I was too busy looking into his eyes. I reached up and tugged at the ear that had been sliced from my head a moment earlier. Then, just as the soldiers were about to drag him away, he asked us, "Why come at night? Why not during the day in the temple courts? But this is your hour," he said turning to the crowd, "the hour when darkness reigns." That's when all his followers ran off into the night.

I remember touching my ear again to make sure I wasn't dreaming. I asked those near me if what had happened to me was real. They nodded in disbelief. The man of miracles had touched me in the hour of darkness.

My blood was still on his fingertips when they led him away.

———————

That night my master and the entire Sanhedrin sentenced the prophet to death. Death? For a man who heals his enemies? *They don't have any evidence against him! He's innocent!*

I wanted to shout it to them, to everyone! But I couldn't—I was just a slave.

They tortured him. They beat him. They whipped him.

And then a few hours later he was dead. *Not this man. Not this way! It isn't right! It can't be happening!*

But it was. I saw it all with my own eyes.

I heard him cry out with my own ears.

And when he died, darkness swallowed everything. Everything.

No! Please, no!

But something deep within me moved. I had a desire to tell my story. The story of when he touched me. The day he died, his story took root in my soul.

———————

Three days later people began to say he was alive again. And I knew it was true— because I'd already begun to change.

You see, even though I was a slave, when he touched me, for the first time in my life I began to feel free. I'll never forget looking into his eyes. Instead of accusing me, they pardoned me. Once you've been touched by this man, no one can ever truly enslave you again.

Have you met him? Has he touched you? Have you looked into his eyes? The hour of darkness is over, and a new day has dawned for all of us who have.

making it personal

> And one of them struck the servant of the high priest,
> cutting off his right ear.
> But Jesus answered, "No more of this!"
> And he touched the man's ear and healed him.
> —Luke 22:50-51

We don't know exactly what happened to the man Jesus healed that night in the garden. We don't know if he ever became a follower of Jesus, a brother of the Son, a part of God's family. We know his name (Malchus) and his job (slave, see John 18:10)—but that's about all.

And we also know that this man was the last person Jesus healed. In fact, it appears he was the last person Jesus ever touched. The last act Jesus did before he was tied up and led away to be killed was to heal one of the men who'd come to lead him to his death. That was the kind of man Jesus was.

And when Jesus died, Malchus's blood was still on his hands. After all, they didn't take Jesus to the washroom on his way to the cross.

I find it hard to believe that this slave's life was the same from then on. I can't help but think that when Jesus touched him, he was changed forever from the inside out.

But I might be wrong.

Lots of people today have been touched by Jesus. Some have been healed physically, others emotionally or spiritually. Jesus still touches lives. And he still changes people. He still sets them free. I've seen people who were set free by Jesus, who were forgiven by him and given the wings to rise above the doldrums of daily life. But then after a while, they drifted back into slavery. They went back to their old chains. You've probably seen it, too.

Instead of living in the freedom of forgiveness and the love of the Son, they go back to their old masters of pornography, or envy, or gossiping, or pride. They go back to the beds of their girl-friends, back to their cheat sheets for the next exam, back to their grudges and lies and excuses. And rather than rising above the temptations that surround them, they immerse themselves in the same old sins once again. Instead of living in the dawn of a new day, they return to the darkness. In fact, I haven't just met people like that. I've been one of them myself.

What about you?

If you haven't met Jesus yet, look into his eyes. You'll find freedom there. You'll find just what you're looking for. Or maybe you have believed in him, but you've drifted back into habits from your old life just like I have—just like we all do.

So what now? What do we do when we realize that we've wandered back into the darkness? Gone back to our old masters? That we've lost sight of the light and enslaved ourselves once again?

There's only one thing to do: Look into his eyes again. Feel his touch again. Receive his forgiveness again. See his smile again. Let him restore you and change you from a slave to a child of God. Again. And again. And again.

He'll do it. He has promised to do it. And the Nazarene always keeps his promises.

taking it deeper

1. How do you think Malchus's life was affected by meeting Jesus? Do you think he changed? Why or why not?

2. Where do you fit into Malchus's story? Have you met the Son? Have you looked into his eyes? Have you seen the forgiveness he offers and believed in him? If so, how will you follow him out of the darkness?

3. Malchus was a slave; he served Caiaphas. What's the name of your master? Is it Jesus? Or is it pornography? Gossiping? Popularity? Masturbation? Drugs? Image? Your body? Cold, hard cash?

4. In what ways do you serve those other masters in your life? In what ways do you serve Jesus? Is it even possible to have two masters? (Hint: Look up Luke 16:13 to see what Jesus has to say about serving two masters.)

5. Read the words of Jesus in Luke 11:21-26. According to Jesus, if we're not fighting for him, what are we doing (see verse 23)? Whose side are you fighting on? How can you tell?

6. When it comes to Jesus, there is no neutral territory. We're either on his side of or on the side of the adversary. How will knowing this truth affect your life? What changes will it bring to your attitude? To your habits? To your lifestyle?

7. Why do some people go back to the darkness? What draws them? What draws you? What can be done about it?

8. Think of a defining moment when you've either looked into Jesus' eyes or away from them. What happened next in your story? Did Jesus reach out and touch you? Did you let him, or did you draw back out of his reach into the shadows? What will you do about that decision right now?

breaking free

Giver of Hope,
Finder of Lost Souls,
free me from the darkness!
lead me to the light!
i don't want to be lost
in my old ways of thinking
and my old ways of living.
i know i can only have one master in my life.
and today i choose that master.

i choose you.

forgive me for the times i've dabbled in the darkness.
forgive me for the times when
i've gone back to my old masters.
free me from them.
lead me by the hand of your love
to the truth of your words.
for when the Son sets us free, we are free indeed.
and that's the kind of freedom
i need.
amen.

name-calling
CHAPTER THIRTEEN

(Matthew 12:46-50, 13:55-57; Luke 2:41-52; John 7:1-5)

I lived in his stupid shadow my whole life.

It was like I didn't even have a name. All because he was the famous one. The miracle worker. The kid wonder. The prodigy. *"Oh, you're James, the brother of Jesus. THE Jesus? The one we keep hearing about? What's it like to be HIS little brother?"*

It made me sick.

I was about eight years old when Mom and Dad accidentally left him in Jerusalem. He was twelve. And you know what? I was kinda glad it happened. Sure I noticed he wasn't with the family when we headed back home. But I didn't say anything. Let him suffer this time. Let him get in trouble for once.

It was so refreshing to step out of his shadow, even for only a few days. But then, of course, they noticed he was missing and eventually tracked him down in the temple.

So Mom yells at him, of course: "Why have you put your father and me through this? We've been looking all over for you!"

And then he starts talking about how they shouldn't have searched at all 'cause they should have known he'd be—quote—in my Father's house—unquote. Those were his exact words, "in my Father's house." And I'm standing there thinking, *What? They found you in the temple, buddy. That's God's house! Who do you think you are anyway? The Son of God?!*

Mom stared at him for a long time when he said that. But she never again called Joseph his dad. I remember that.

We all knew there was something different about him. And it wasn't just the things he said. It was the way he looked at you. As if he could look inside you and know what was going on in your heart. It was kinda spooky.

I remember one time when I was about ten or eleven. I was with some of my friends, and we found this little girl who could hardly walk. Something was wrong with her legs. We threw rocks at her and teased her and laughed at her till our sides hurt. And when I got home, Jesus just looked at me. I was like, "What?" And he kept looking at me. "What?!" He didn't say anything, but he knew. I could tell he knew. And it was weird. I wanted to apologize—not just to the girl, but to him. Spooky.

And he was strong. Not the kind of guy you'd mess with. I mean, you know how guys are. We're always sizing up the competition to see if we could take 'em or not. There's, like, this pecking order. And the toughest guys rise to the top of the stack. Well, no one messed with him. No one pushed him around. He was tough as nails, but he didn't flaunt it. He had a quiet strength that actually intimidated people. I've never seen anything like it before.

He could have been a good carpenter. I mean, after all those years learning the trade, working with Dad. Mom was so proud of him.

But then one day he just left. He just walked away from the sawdust and the two-by-fours. Just gave up the whole family business to become a revivalist preacher. Can you imagine? If Dad had still been alive, I'll bet he would have been disappointed. Is that how you treat your family? Walk out on them in the prime of your life? He was the firstborn. He was supposed to take care of Mom, but apparently he had other priorities.

So then, when he started in with the miracles and everything, it got even worse. *"Oh, you're James, the brother of Jesus?! The prophet?! The healer? Did he ever do any of those miracles when you were growing up? Huh? Huh? Huh?"*

The answer is no. He never did any of those miracles when we were growing up. Even when he could have. Even when Dad got sick. Even when Dad died. No miracles. Nothing. Just tears like the rest of us.

Then one time he returns home to Nazareth with his little band of merry men. We'd heard about his supposed miracles. Everyone was talking about them. So we said, "All right, Mr. Messiah. We've heard the stories. Let's see the proof. Put your magic where your mouth is." But he couldn't do it. He couldn't pull anything out of his hat—except for healing a few sick people.

"It's your lack of belief," he said, shaking his head. "It astonishes me."

I wanted to say, "It's your claims that are astonishing, buddy. It's this Messiah complex you have. It's not our fault you can't do miracles. It's yours!"

But I didn't say anything because there was something unsettlingly sad in the way he looked at me. It wasn't like he was making excuses. There was something else going on. Something I couldn't quite figure out.

Then he left. And the stories about his miracles got more and more impressive: calming storms, walking on the sea, feeding thousands with a handful of food. And I started wondering, *How does he do it? Tricks? Sleight of hand? Could any of the stories really be true?*

Go figure. The religious leaders wanted to kill him; the regular people wanted to make him king. We all started wondering what it all meant, where everything was going.

———

All I wanted was a little proof, you know? I mean, he was making some pretty wild claims. And people were starting to believe them. To follow him. To worship him. That was the scary thing. They actually worshiped and prayed to my brother.

All I wanted was a little proof.

By the next time I saw him, he wasn't even acting rational anymore. Missing meals so he could teach the people. Staying up all night praying, holding those healing services.

And then there was that one day when we'd finally had enough. The church leaders thought he'd gotten possessed by a demon. Honestly, Mom and I thought he'd lost his mind—that he'd gone completely insane. We couldn't even get into the room, so we discreetly sent word to him, "Your mother and brothers are right outside. C'mon, Jesus, let's go home. Let's get this taken care of."

And what does he say? "Who are my mother and brothers?" Then he looks at those seated in a circle around him and says, "Here are my mother and my brothers! Whoever does God's will is my brother and sister and mother!"

I saw the look on Mom's face when he said that. Pain. Like a sword in her soul. I could just imagine what she was thinking: *What did I do wrong? Where did I mess up? Whatever happened to my nice, respectable boy?*

And all I could think was, *I'm your brother, Jesus! Don't you hear me?! And that's your mom! Not these strangers! This is your own flesh and blood here! I'm your brother! Haven't you ever noticed that? Don't you understand who you are?!*

Things spun out of control pretty quickly after that. The arrest. The trial. The beatings. I was there that day. I saw it all. I didn't look away.

After all, he was my brother.

I watched my big brother die on a cross. I heard the things people said about him while he was hanging there. And I wanted to say, "Hey, shut up! That's my brother up there! My brother!" But I was afraid. I didn't say anything.

He did this deal on the cross where he told John—one of his friends—to be Mom's son. "This is your son," he said to her. "This is your mom," he said to John. Then he looked my way . . .

Why didn't he say that to me?

Because all your life you've been ashamed of him . . .

The words cut through me.

You were ashamed of him . . . You never believed . . .

A couple of his friends took his body down. Mom cried a lot that day. I stayed with her, trying to console her. But I really didn't know what to say.

As odd as he was, as wild as his claims might have been, he didn't deserve to die. Not like that.

He was my brother . . . He'd always been my brother . . .

And then, on that Sunday morning, Mary Magdalene came bolting into town with the news.

"Alive," she said, trying to catch her breath. "He's alive again!"

Of course, we couldn't believe it. I mean, sure, we remembered some of the stuff he'd said. Some of the claims he'd made. But they couldn't really be true . . . could they?

"I saw him myself!" she exclaimed.

There had to be some kind of mistake. Maybe someone had stolen his body.

"Mary, tell me what happened," I said.

She looked me straight in the eyes. She grabbed my hands as she spoke. "I saw him, James. By the grave." Her voice trembled with excitement. "At first I thought it was the groundskeeper, but then he called me by name. It was him. It was Jesus! And he told me, 'Don't be afraid. Go to my brothers and tell them, "I'm returning to my Father and your Father, to my God and your God." Go and tell them. Go and tell them all!' It was him, James! He's alive again!"

Go and tell my brothers? . . . I'm returning to my Father and your Father? . . . To my God and your God?

To my God?

To my Father?

Suddenly, everything I'd known, everything I'd ever believed about him began to unravel. All the times I'd judged him . . . looked down on him . . . resented him. I started shaking.

I had to sit down. Could it be? Could he really be alive again? Could he really have been telling the truth all along?

"Yes."

I heard a voice whisper in my soul.

"Yes, James."

His voice.

"Yes, my brother. It's true."

Suddenly, I seemed to awaken as if from a long sleep. I began to understand. In that moment I finally realized who he really was. And who I really am. It was something he'd known all along, something he'd been trying to tell me for years. But I'd never been ready to hear it. And I'd never really grasped it until then.

Who am I? That's a good question.

I am James.

And I am the brother of Jesus.

making it personal

> "He's just a carpenter's son, and we know Mary, his mother,
> and his brothers—James, Joseph, Simon, and Judas.
> All his sisters live right here among us. What makes him so great?"
> And they were deeply offended and refused to believe in him.
> —Matthew 13:55-57(NLT)

Put yourself in James's shoes for a minute. Imagine having Jesus as your older brother. Think of what it would have been like to try to live up to that reputation! Everyone would always be comparing you to him. To his behavior in school. His grades. His character. His life.

Imagine it.

Ouch.

Now think about this: Why did it take James so long to recognize Jesus for who he truly was? I mean, c'mon! Jesus was God wrapped up in human form! And his family lived with him year after year. His brothers saw him at home and at work and at school and at play, with his hair down and his guard down. And yet for the longest time they didn't have a clue who he really was. They didn't get it. They didn't believe.

Actually, now that I think about it, the same thing happens today. People grow up hearing about Jesus. That he was a great man. A miracle worker. An enlightened spiritual teacher. But they never understand that he came to earth to enter our human family so that we could be reborn into his divine family. They think of following Jesus as some type of religion, but he never talked about it in those terms. Instead Jesus talked about spiritual life as a relationship in which you're reborn as a child of God.

When we place our faith in Jesus, we become children of the Father and siblings of the Son—adopted into the family of faith through Jesus Christ (Ephesians 1:5).

And, yes, people will naturally compare you to Jesus when they find out that you're part of his family. Because it really is just as

Jesus said, "For whoever does the will of my Father in heaven is my brother and sister and mother" (Matthew 12:50).

So here's the question: When people see you, will they notice the family resemblance? "Hey, you really remind me of your big brother. You two are so much alike! I can hardly tell the two of you apart."

I hope so, because then you can smile and say, "Thanks. Wanna join the family?"

taking it deeper

1. Jesus said that those who do the will of God are his true brothers and sisters. Jesus' brother James eventually became a respected leader of the church in Jerusalem. Most scholars also believe he wrote the book of James in the Bible. Read James 1:22; 2:14-17, 26; and 4:17. Did James take Jesus' words to heart?

2. People are quick to compare us to others—whether it's to our brothers and sisters, our classmates, or other members of our sports teams. Has that ever happened to you? How does it make you feel?

3. Read John 3:16. How does it make you feel to know that God accepts you "as is" and loves you just the way you are? How does knowing that God loves you unconditionally change the way you see yourself?

4. Jesus never once told people to be more religious. Why do you think that is? What did he tell them instead? (See John 8:34-36.)

5. Jesus said that no one comes to him unless the Father draws him or her (John 6:44). Is God drawing you? If so, what are you going to do? Fight him or follow him? Don't try too hard to define how it feels or to figure out if you're being religious enough, or spiritual enough, or something like that. Read 1 Peter 1:8. How will faith in God affect your life?

6. Is your heart being stirred to believe? If so, the Father is draw-

ing you. Don't pull away. Let him adopt you into the family of the Son. Will you believe and become a child of God today?

7. Check out Ephesians 1:4-7. What do these verses have to say about God's plan for your life and your relationship with God the moment you believe?

8. Adoption never depends on your effort. It's a relationship (John 1:12-13). Read Romans 8:15. How does our adoption into God's family change the way we should look at God?

breaking free

Jesus,
i want you to be my brother.
and i want to live like you're my brother.
i mean it, really live it out.

i want to be part of the family of God. forever.
i know it doesn't depend on me—
on my effort or anything,
but on your grace and forgiveness.
well, here i am.
help me to believe,
and to overcome my doubts.

draw me in. adopt me into your family, Jesus.
i can't wait to go home.
amen.

waking the dead
CHAPTER FOURTEEN

(Mark 5:21-43; 1 Corinthians 15:3-6)

It isn't the blood that bothers me the most. Or even the smell. It's seeing the families when the moment comes. That's always the toughest part for me.

Sometimes they just can't stop screaming. Sometimes they shake and shiver as one wave of tears after another grabs hold of them. Sometimes they pound the walls or pound each other. They collapse on the floor. They get that lost look in their eyes and just stand there trembling. Powerless. Hopeless.

From that first ear-piercing wail to the tired, tearless, bloodshot eyes, it's the hardest part of my job.

Sometimes the little kids laugh. They don't understand. "He's only sleeping, Mommy," they say. "Don't worry. He'll wake up." They're too young to understand.

Most adults can't accept it right away, either. They deny it. They convince themselves it'll all go away. They pretend it's not real. And then suddenly, the realization sinks in. The light drains out of their eyes. Horror seeps in.

When I see that, I have to look away.

Even though I'm not 20 yet, I've been through it all dozens of times. Because it's my job to be there. To help the family grieve. To breathe the music of their pain.

Ever since I was a little girl, I've had an ear for music. When my mom noticed it, back when I was about five, she arranged for me to take flute lessons.

At weddings I play tunes of joy. At funerals I play songs of pain.

They always walk us past the corpse so we can see it for ourselves, so we can give a clearer voice to their grief. That's never easy, either.

I especially hate it when it's a kid.

I always look at them, thinking, *She was only eight . . . or ten . . . or two . . . I've already lived ten years or eight years or sixteen years longer than she ever will . . . that could've been you lying there, Rachel . . . that could've been you . . .*

Then I close my eyes and lift my flute to my lips. And I begin to play. The music fills the room. The mourners join the song. The whisper of my flute and the pain of their cries blend together into a lament that lets everyone in the town know what has happened.

Some of the mourners are family members, of course. But if the family is rich enough, they'll hire professional mourners to help comfort them, to give voice to their grief.

Weeping. Wailing. Crying. Shouting. Sometimes they'll tear their clothes apart, pull their own hair out, or smear ashes on their faces to show the depth of their grief. We don't hide pain around here.

I guess in some cultures it might seem odd to make such a public display of our pain. But not to us. Instead of wearing black or hiding our tears or speaking in hushed tones, we let loose. We let our sorrow slash through us and land in the streets. We don't hide death here. And there's something healthy about that.

But the mourners and musicians don't really feel the family's grief. I mean, of course we're sad. But it's one thing to cry, and it's another to grieve. You can pay someone to cry in front of you, but you can't hire them to feel your tears. You can pay someone to play a song for you, but you can't hire them to know your heart. Crying is one thing. Grieving is another. Grieving is something you have to do alone.

So a few months ago I was preparing lunch with my mom when the door burst open. The messenger was out of breath. "He asked for you," the man gasped. "Before going to find the healer, he asked for you. She's not getting any better. You might be needed," he paused and then added, "before lunch."

I nodded slowly. I'd been expecting this. I set down the dough I was kneading and wiped off my hands. My mother lowered her eyes. She was used to me running out like this; she knew what it meant. I grabbed my flute and headed for the door.

The messenger was from the family of Jairus, the ruler of our synagogue. Jairus was the kind of man who would sit with families for days or weeks in their time of loss, praying and fasting for them. And he would never complain about it. But now it was his daughter who was sick—his only daughter.

She'd been going downhill for the last two weeks. Every time she seemed to be getting better, every time the family got their hopes up again, the fever would return worse than before.

In the last couple of days her breathing had become ragged and weak. All of us knew she wouldn't last long.

As I approached the house, I could hear the mourners shrieking with sorrow. Their cries told me all I needed to know.

Apparently, Jairus didn't even know yet. As I walked in the door, two servants were leaving. I guess they were hoping to find him before he brought the healer over.

So while they went to look for the father, we went to look at the girl.

I walked up the stairs slowly. I could hear the mother and a few of the mourners in the room at the top of the stairs. Their wails ripped through me. So hopeless. So raw. So fierce with pain. There's nothing as heartbreaking as the sound of a mother's cry when she kneels beside her dead child.

Quietly, I entered the room and looked at the girl. Her eyes were closed. Her chest was still, her face pale. I knew that if I touched her hand, it would feel like cool meat and not warm flesh. I knew because back when I first began playing at funerals, I would touch the hands just to make sure. But I stopped doing that long ago. The feel of cold clay would haunt me.

No, I don't touch the hands anymore.

I'd heard she was 12, but she was small for her age. Her dark hair hung still and thick, cascading off her mat and onto the floor like a frozen waterfall. Frozen in time. Frozen in death.

A lump rose in my throat.

I hate it when it's a kid.

As I looked at the body, I saw a crimson bead oozing out of the corner of her mouth. No one else had seen it yet. I couldn't stand the thought of the mother looking up and seeing that rose-red blood staining her daughter's face. So I gently wiped the dead girl's mouth with the sleeve of my dress and placed my other hand on the shoulder of the shaking, crumpled mother to try to comfort her. I don't think it worked. Her sobs didn't quiet down.

Then, with the dead girl's blood drying on my sleeve, I went back downstairs with the others. I pulled out my flute and began to play a song full of tears and blood and death. It was one of the saddest songs I'd ever played.

We'd been at it for almost an hour when they arrived.

I saw them approaching through the window: Jairus, the servants, and—what's this?—the healer and some of his followers, all silently walking up to the door.

The healer had come? But why? To offer a prayer, maybe? To comfort the family?

As he entered the house and saw us, his voice rose above the cries of even the loudest mourners. "Stop! Quiet! What are you doing?"

Slowly, the sound of weeping died down until all was silent in the house.

I pulled the flute from my lips and looked around. We all looked at him.

"This girl isn't dead," he said firmly. "She's only asleep."

The room was silent for a moment longer, but that was all. One of the younger mourners lost it first. It started as a snicker in the back of the room. Then it spread among the mourners, a series of giggles, a ripple of laughter. Not the clean kind of laughter you let out after a good joke, but the rotten kind of laughter that seeps out when you're making fun of someone. You know the kind of laughter I mean.

I'm ashamed to admit it, but I laughed with the others. Softly, not as loud as some of them, but I laughed, too. We knew she wasn't asleep. The girl was dead.

And because I knew that, I laughed.

Of course, the parents and servants didn't laugh. They stood there in shock, quivering slightly. They didn't laugh. No, of course they didn't laugh. Love wouldn't let them laugh. But we weren't being paid to love the girl, just to help the family grieve for her.

So in that tragic, horrible moment, we laughed.

"Get out of here. All of you, get out!" He threw open the door with a bang. Then he pointed to a few of his friends. "You, Peter, John, James. Come with me."

But the girl was dead . . . What was he doing?

waking the dead

"Outside," he repeated. "Now!"

Some of the other mourners had set their jaws. Some were sneering. But slowly, they began to file out the door.

I didn't know what to do. Finally, I set my flute on a shelf near the stairs so I could find it easily when he let us back in to finish our work. Then I stepped outside into the late afternoon sunlight to wait with the others.

For a few minutes some of the girls kept giggling until one of the older ladies shushed them. Someone said something about how she'd better still get paid. Then it was pretty much quiet.

None of the mourners were crying anymore.

What was he doing in there? Why did they bring the healer here when the girl was already dead? Why did he want to be alone with the body? And why on earth would he say she was only asleep?

"Huh! Does he want I should stand around here all day?" announced one lady suddenly. "I'm going home."

Another woman nodded. "If he wants to make jokes about a dead girl, I'm going home, too."

But he hadn't been joking. That much I knew for sure. It wasn't a joke.

The crowd of mourners began to shrink as the women headed home.

I just stood there. Should I wait or go? The sound of our sour laughter rang in my head. It sounded even worse than the manufactured tears.

It wasn't right, but what could I do? Nothing. I couldn't do anything. The girl was dead, and the healer didn't want us here. So I should probably go back home and help my mother finish baking the bread.

But I couldn't leave without my flute. I had to go back in and get it.

I eased the door open and stepped inside. It took a moment for my eyes to adjust to the dim light. The house was eerily silent. It didn't even sound like the parents were crying upstairs.

I crossed the room softly, and just as I reached for my flute, I heard a loud gasp from the top of the staircase.

Then a shout.

Then a squeal.

"Daughter! My daughter!" It was the voice of the dead girl's mother. "You're back! You're alive!"

What?!

A moment later a cluster of people emerged from the room at the top of the stairs.

And as they did, a chill grabbed my spine.

No! It can't be!

A ghost. The ghost of the girl floating beside her father.

No!

My eyes were playing tricks on me. My eyes had to be playing tricks on me!

I staggered backward, clutching my flute.

She saw me. "Shalom!" she called: Peace!

Ghosts don't smile and wish you blessings and peace.

"Shalom!" she said again. And I knew she was no ghost. She waved at me. The girl I'd been hired to help mourn was coming down the stairs. Not only was she alive, but the sickness was gone. She was walking around!

I mouthed the word, "Shalom," but no sound came out.

The healer's three friends were staring at me from the top of the stairs. The girl's mother and father were there, too. All of them looked as stunned as I did. Then Jesus, the healer, stepped out of the room and looked at me.

"I . . . I forgot my flute," I whispered. I thought maybe he would be angry at me for coming back into the house. "I'm sorry. I didn't—"

"It's okay," he said softly. "But you mustn't tell anyone what you saw. All of you. Do you understand me? You must not tell a soul."

I nodded slowly. So did the others.

He pointed at me. "Promise me. Not a word."

"I . . . I . . . "

"Promise me."

"I promise," I said.

"Good. Now go on home, Rachel. And not a word, even to your mother."

What? How did he know my name? How did he know my mother?!

I nodded. I still hadn't taken my eyes off the girl.

And as I backed my way out the front door, I heard Jesus laugh a little—a clear, clean laugh. "Jairus, give your daughter something to eat. The time for mourning is over."

As I stepped into the afternoon sunlight, everything seemed surreal. Like a dream. The funeral. The girl. Maybe I was asleep. Maybe that was it. Maybe I was dreaming . . .

Then I noticed the sleeve of my dress smeared with blood. A dead girl's blood. A dead girl who was no longer dead. I touched it. It was real. It was all real.

But how?!

People had been saying that the healer came from God, from heaven itself . . . and there was no other explanation. He must have!

How else could he have done it? He brought a dead girl back to life! They were right!

Oh, I had to tell someone! I had to tell everyone!

But I'd promised not to say a word.

Needless to say, in the end I couldn't help it. I didn't keep my promise.

I just couldn't keep the news to myself. How could I not tell the story? And naturally, word spread like wildfire. As soon as the other women who'd been there saw the girl at the market the next day, the whole town knew. The whole region did.

Jesus had brought a dead girl back to life!

And we had laughed at him when he went in to awaken her.

It bothered me that I hadn't kept my promise to him. At first I didn't understand why he'd told us to be quiet. It didn't make any sense to me.

At first.

But then, as time wore on and his reputation grew, he had to start avoiding the crowds. He had to stop teaching in some areas altogether. I began to see that fame was his enemy. It wasn't what he wanted. Then the angry politicians and rulers rose against him. They claimed he was a threat to our religion and our way of life. Things were spinning out of control. His fame was strangling his ministry. And I knew I was partly to blame. First I'd laughed at him. Then I'd lied to him. And now he was in trouble.

I remember thinking, *What have I done? I never meant to hurt him! I believe in him. I really do! After what he did, I'd believe anything he said. But I've hurt him by what I did!*

I wanted to apologize, but of course I didn't get a chance to talk to him. Then came his trial . . . his conviction . . . his crucifixion.

I never got the chance to say I was sorry. And I couldn't help but feel that it was partly my fault that he was hanging there, dying on that cross. After all, I'd done the opposite of what he wanted, what he asked of me. And they'd caught him, and now they were killing him.

This man who could awaken the dead was dying.

The politicians and priests laughed at him as he hung there struggling for breath.

I recognized their kind of laughter.

I cried that day—real tears, not manufactured ones. I was grieving then. For real.

As darkness swept over the land, I saw his mother kneeling at the foot of the cross, crying before the cooling corpse of her son.

A mother's cry. The fiercest pain of all.

No one was asked to play at his death. No one was asked to mourn.

I climb the hill and look around. Lots of other people are already gathered. Dozens of us, hundreds, maybe. All waiting expectantly.

I'm trembling slightly, filled with fear and hope. Such a strange combination. Fear because I feel guilty. And hope that maybe, just maybe, it's true.

The rumors have been circulating for a couple of weeks now. Here's what we know for sure—they buried him, sealed the tomb, and set a guard. But during the weekend the body disappeared. No one knew where it was. And within a few days his followers were telling people they'd seen him again. Alive. Back from the dead.

So now, on this day, we've gathered. To see for ourselves.

Jairus and his daughter are here. She's laughing and running with her friends and smiling and letting the sunlight dance across her face.

She waves to me.

"Shalom!"

"Shalom," I say.

"You came to play for me!" she says. And I don't know what to say. I want to tell her that I laughed about her death, but I can't seem to. I want to say I'm sorry that I spread the news, that I played my part in sending her healer to die, but I don't.

"Yes," I say at last, waving my flute in her direction. I'm doing my best to sound happy. "I played for you when you were dead."

A moment later the air around me seems to split open.

And as we gasp, he appears.

We drop to our knees, but he tells us to get up. We want to bow at his feet, but he opens his arms to hug us instead. The children are the first ones to run to him. They're not afraid.

But I am. I wait. I hang in the back of the pack.

Finally, he turns to me.

"I know you," he says. And he draws me into his arms. He is no ghost. He is real.

I'm shaking. I know what I have to say. But I struggle with the words. It takes me three tries. Fear chokes me.

"I . . . I laughed," I say at last.

"I know," he says.

"And I . . . I . . . I told. I know you didn't want me to tell, but I did. I couldn't keep it to myself."

"I know."

I want so badly for him to accept me even though I've let him down.

Finally, I manage to whisper the words that have been tearing away at my soul. "I'm sorry," I whisper. By then I'm crying.

"Yes," he says, "I know."

Then he takes both of my hands and looks me right in the eyes. His hands aren't cool like clay—they're warm and invitingly alive. "I'm not angry with you, Rachel. I chose the cross. Now don't cry."

He wipes my tears away, touching my cheek as softly as a melody. "This time you can tell," he says to me in an urgent whisper. "This time I want you to tell. Tell everyone."

"Tell them?"

"Yes. Tell the story. The time has come."

"Oh, Jesus," I stammer, "I will."

And this time I'll keep my promise. I really will. I'll share the story, the mystery of it all. I'll tell his story and play the song of life so even those who weren't there that day can meet him for themselves. So they can meet the living, breathing Mystery for themselves. For he didn't just awaken that girl. He didn't just awaken himself. He also awakened me.

"And now," he says with a wide grin. "Before I go home, how about a little song? Something lively. Something we can really dance to."

I nod and lift my flute to my lips.

And I begin to play.

making it personal

When Jesus entered the ruler's house and saw the flute players and the noisy crowd, he said, "Go away. The girl is not dead but asleep." But they laughed at him. After the crowd had been put outside, he went in and took the girl by the hand, and she got up. News of this spread through all that region.

—Matthew 9:23-26

To humans, death appears to be the end because we look at it from one side of the mirror. But to Jesus, death is a doorway that can swing both ways. To him, waking the dead is as easy as rousing someone from a late afternoon nap.

That's why he called death "sleep." To him, the only thing permanent about death is the judgment that follows it.

And it isn't just the physically dead that Jesus is an expert at awakening. According to Ephesians 2:1-2, all of us are dead in a much deeper, more spiritual sense: "As for you, you were dead in your transgressions and sins, in which you used to live when you followed the ways of this world." Our spiritual selves need to be awakened. For all of us have followed the ways of the world.

Before we can enter heaven, each one of us needs to be brought back from the dead. As John writes, "Now this is eternal life: that they may know you, the only true God, and Jesus Christ, whom you have sent" (John 17:3). Getting to know Jesus is the only way to receive eternal life.

If you've never experienced that new life, it's not too late. Turn to him. Believe in him. You'll never be the same again. The time for mourning is over.

The time for dancing has arrived.

taking it deeper

1. Imagine that you were there that day at the funeral when Jesus said the girl was only asleep. Would you have laughed? Why or why not? What does the mourners' laughter say about their faith in Jesus?

2. We know that after seeing some of his miracles, people put their faith in Jesus. (See John 11:43-45.) What would it take for you to believe in Jesus?

3. Read 1 Corinthians 15:3-6. According to these verses, how many people saw Jesus after he rose from the dead? Think of the people you've met in this book. Which ones do you think might have been there? Why?

waking the dead

4. Throughout most of 1 Corinthians 15, Paul emphasizes the importance of Jesus' physical resurrection. In verses 17-20, what does he say would be the result if Jesus hadn't really come back from the dead?

5. According to 1 Corinthians 15:54-56, what has happened to death? What assurances do these verses give you? How vital is the resurrection of Jesus Christ to your life today?

6. Read John 11:25-26. What light does this verse shed on life, death, and eternity? What do you think Jesus meant when he said, "I am the resurrection"? He didn't say he simply would rise, but that he himself was the rising of the dead. What do you think he meant?

7. According to Matthew 28:18-20, right before Jesus went to heaven, what did he ask his followers to do? Do you think these verses apply to your life today? Explain.

8. Read Acts 1:8-9. How do these two verses relate to what you just read in Matthew? Has the Holy Spirit come upon you? Are you Jesus' witness, too? How will this story and these first-century words of Jesus affect your life today, in the 21st century?

9. If Jesus walked up to you as he did to the flute player in the story after he came back from the dead, what would you say to him? What do you need to say to him right now?

breaking free

O Waker of the Dead,
awaken me.

find the faith in my soul that is as dead as night;
find the hope in my heart that is as dry as dust;
find the love in my spirit that is so fast asleep.
    peer beneath the shroud of my life
and awaken me.
look deeply, Jesus.
    find the child there,
    find the dreamer there,

find the lover there.
awaken me.

you are the one who has conquered the grave,
you are the one who has tasted new life.
help me die to the dying life,
    and live to the life that never dies
by entering the mystery of your love.
right here. right now. today.
amen.